The

Mocha

MANUAL

to Turning Your

PASSION into PROFIT

Also by Kimberly Seals-Allers

**The Mocha Manual
to a Fabulous Pregnancy**

The

Mocha
MANUAL

to Turning Your

PASSION into PROFIT

✳

How to Find and Grow Your Side Hustle
in Any Economy

✳

Kimberly Seals-Allers

Amistad
An Imprint of HarperCollins*Publishers*

THE MOCHA MANUAL TO TURNING YOUR PASSION INTO PROFIT. Copyright © 2009 by Kimberly Seals-Allers. All rights reserved. Printed in the United States of America. No part of this book may be used or reproduced in any manner whatsoever without written permission except in the case of brief quotations embodied in critical articles and reviews. For information address HarperCollins Publishers, 10 East 53rd Street, New York, NY 10022.

HarperCollins books may be purchased for educational, business, or sales promotional use. For information please write: Special Markets Department, HarperCollins Publishers, 10 East 53rd Street, New York, NY 10022.

FIRST EDITION

Designed by Susan Yang

Library of Congress Cataloging-in-Publication Data has been applied for.

ISBN 978-0-06-143849-3

09 10 11 12 13 WBC/RRD 10 9 8 7 6 5 4 3 2 1

To my children,

Kayla & Michael Jaden,

who fuel my passion for life

Contents

Acknowledgments

Many, many thanks to the countless people who supported me to complete this book. First and foremost, I thank Jehovah for giving me the strength to get through difficult times. My second debt of gratitude goes to the many women, entrepreneurs, trailblazers, and superstars who shared their stories, triumphs, and struggles with me to make this book possible. To my parents, James and Alma Seals, I am eternally grateful for your love and support. Katrina, Jeffrey, Aunt Margretta, and Naelen, thank you for always believing in me and telling me I could do it even when I didn't think so. Thanks to Tamika Nunley and Christen Claytor for your research assistance and for helping me stay organized—a thankless job, I know. And to Dawn Davis, my book editor, thank you for believing in me and the Mocha Manual brand and pushing me to give you my best. Thanks to my girlfriends, Donna, Sherese, Schalawn, and Keiva, who helped with babysitting, inspirational bottles of wine to help ease the writer's block, comedic relief, and so much more throughout this project—I value our friendship.

Lastly, I want to thank my children, Kayla and Michael Jaden, for reminding me to laugh, showing me the true meaning of love, and helping me soar to new heights. And to Greg, my chief cheerleader and partner in life—I couldn't have done it without you.

The

Mocha

MANUAL

to Turning Your

PASSION into PROFIT

You Can Turn Your Side Hustle into the Life of Your Dreams

Our deepest fear is not that we are inadequate. Our
deepest fear is that we are powerful beyond measure.
It is our light not our darkness that most frightens us.
We ask ourselves, who am I to be brilliant, gorgeous,
talented and fabulous. Actually, who are you *not* to be?
—*Marianne Williamson*

I am an entrepreneur. This may sound like an easy and
simple declaration. But my road to entrepreneurship was a
long and winding one. You see, for most of my working life
I have always been connected to something bigger than myself—a
major magazine, a large media company, or a high-circulation
daily newspaper—and unbeknownst to me, this was a huge part of
my self-identity. The mere thought of leaving that security and
all that comes from being connected to something bigger than
life was far too scary for me to take on. Today, I'm the president
of the Mocha Manual Company—the preeminent voice, advisor,
and ally of the woman of color market. I have the amazing honor
of working each day doing what I love—I am passionate and I am told
it shows! A great deal of my time is spent editing and directing

Mocha Manual dot com which has quickly become a favorite resource and an active, lively community for mothers of color on the Web. There I get to offer vibrant and informative content, connect women with each other, share my picks for the best maternity and infant wear and gifts, and more. I also consult a range of companies who target the women of color market— sharing my unique insights and expertise on this exceptional segment of women (us!). My fast-growing international company was born out of the success of my first book, *The Mocha Manual to a Fabulous Pregnancy*, and my deep passion for pregnancy and motherhood. *The Mocha Manual to a Fabulous Pregnancy* DVD is nationally distributed at Wal-Mart and other national retailers. And as you can see from this savvy purchase in your hands right now, the Mocha Manual line of books is expanding to address the whole journey of a black woman's life.

That is now. Just a few years ago, the very thought of stepping out on my own and having no steady paycheck to rely on sounded more like something worthy of the final round of *Fear Factor*. Even starting a business on the side was frightening. Many times I had to invest money that I couldn't necessarily spare or give up sleep and my free time on the weekends to get my venture off the ground.

This is the life of the side hustler. We work our nine-to-five and then we go to work again for ourselves. Taking that side hustle to the next level, however, is a greater challenge. The thought of your side hustle being your only hustle and a thriving, money-earning, bill-paying business often seems like a far-fetched dream. To achieve this requires more energy, money, time, or other resources than you currently have. Or so it seems. Another big obstacle is fear. All of this is real and human and part of the journey. But when you have a map of how to get somewhere, it immediately seems that much more attainable. When you know that someone who looks like you and comes from where you come from has done it successfully, you're empowered to make it happen for yourself! That's what *The Mocha Manual to Turning Your Passion into Profit* is all about.

If you are reading this book, then congratulations are in order. You want something more out of your life! To get there, you are probably among the growing cadre of women who are using their personal interests as a springboard into entrepreneurship and a life of greater fulfillment and purpose. According to the National Foundation for Women Business Owners (NFWBO), 14 percent of women business owners in the United States have turned a personal interest into a working business.

Black women are a big part of this statistic. In fact, black women are more likely than women of other races to be business owners. According to the National Women's Business Council, black females own nearly half a million businesses, employing more than 250,000 people and generating nearly $20 billion in sales. During my years as a senior editor at *Essence,* I saw firsthand the unbelievable number of black women who are working a side hustle and stepping into entrepreneurship. It was mind boggling. In fact, I am unequivocally convinced that at the heart of every black woman is the soul of a hustler. Jay-Z ain't got nothing on us. We can work a demanding professional job every day and then swing a side business or two after hours and on the weekends. If you look around your own sister circle, I'm sure there are one or two friends, at least, who are doing something extra on the side. It's an undeniable trend among black women.

Those side hustles are helping us edge out white women in the earnings race. According to the 2003 census report, black women with bachelor's degrees typically earned $41,000 annually, compared to $37,800 for a white woman and $43,700 for a college-educated Asian woman. Sociologists and economists have attributed this increase to our likelihood to have more than one job or to somehow earn extra income on the side. Even they know how we do! Economists also note that since blacks suffered more financially as a result of the 2001 recession and its aftermath, black women, who are predominantly the breadwinners in their families, have had to get their hustle on, so to speak, to make ends meet and help black households financially recover.

What else is behind this increase in black women tapping into their inner hustler? Sure, there's the opportunity to earn extra cash and pay bills. Or the lure of a surplus stash to fund a little splurge every month. But for the majority of black women, a side hustle is an expression of our passion and life's purpose even if we have a financially rewarding nine-to-five. There are countless other black women with side hustles who have successfully scaled corporate ladders and proven that we can play and win at "their" game. In fact, according to the National Women's Business Council, 14.9 percent of black female business owners have a master's or other advanced degree, compared to 15.2 percent of white and 9 percent of Latina business owners. So we've got our papers! But we want it all—we want success *and* personal fulfillment. And while our professional jobs give us a sense of accomplishment, our side hustles fulfill our passions.

For me, my purpose in life is to empower women of color to have healthy pregnancies and to support mothers in one of the most important journeys of life. You see, we plan our careers with our minds, being fully strategic and making "smart" decisions. But we start our side hustles from our heart, doing something that makes us feel empowered, whole, and fully self-expressed. What if you could follow your heart *and* fill your bank account regardless of the economic climate? What if you could be fulfilled and financially rewarded? What if you could get past whatever stops you from taking the plunge into the life of a full-time entrepreneur? What if there was a guidebook created just for you that showed you how to overcome emotional obstacles, brush up on your business skills, and create a plan to turn your passion into a profitable business and financial freedom?

To do so, we've got some work to do. Despite our record-breaking numbers as entrepreneurs, our business revenues significantly lag behind those of other ethnicities. According to a recent report by the U.S. Small Business Administration's Women's Business Council, companies owned and led by black women average annual receipts of $41,000 per year, versus $175,000 for whites, $74,000 for Latinas, and $185,000 for Asians. We've got the passion, but we need to boost the profits!

This is the purpose of *The Mocha Manual to Turning Your Passion into Profit*. Yes, as you read you'll be motivated to move past your fears and get in touch with your purpose and passion. But more important, you'll learn the business mechanics, strategies, and secrets of what it takes to turn a profit and create a sustainable and fast-growing enterprise. You'll even meet several women with million-dollar businesses built from scratch. Ultimately, you will be guided through the process of creating a workable transitional plan to full self-employment. This book is for any black woman who wants to start a small business and take greater financial control of her life!

Using real-life stories, personal anecdotes, and actionable advice, this prescriptive guide shares proven strategies and principles that lead to business success and personal fulfillment in your work. You'll read real-life stories of successful black women who started with nothing and ended up with a money-earning side hustle that allowed them to eventually leave their nine-to-five job, grow their business into a money-earning enterprise, and ultimately profit from their passion. I'll share my lessons learned working nearly two decades as an award-winning business journalist, along with my school-of-hard-knocks lessons from building the Mocha Manual into a multinational multimedia brand. This book offers a host of creative ideas for making money, priceless principles that lead to success, specific steps to structure and build a side hustle, marketing advice on how to get your business noticed, key elements for increasing sales, and a blueprint for creating a transitional plan that turns your side hustle into your only hustle.

It is not revolutionary that we are returning to self-sufficiency by doing what we love. Before industrialization sent hordes of us to the cities to work on assembly lines in factories, we all traded something we did or owned in exchange for the things we couldn't do or didn't own. Experts say that before the Industrial Revolution, 80 percent of us were entrepreneurs. And not so long ago, when we weren't allowed to have real jobs in fancy offices, our ancestors made their own way out of no way.

But it is somewhat revolutionary that we are now so empowered that after having been taught to follow the rules our whole lives, we are escaping this conformist structure and creating new rules, new ideals of success. In our community, so many black women have played the office game well to achieve the so-called symbols of success. But when they made it to the top of the ladder or to one of the higher rungs, there was still something missing. There was little fulfillment. As it turns out, we were playing their game when deep down we really wanted to play a different game—a game where we win on our terms, not theirs. So after proving that, yeah, we could do that, we are now empowered to walk away from the things our parents call "good jobs" and create our own definition of success, to create a life that gives us fulfillment and a paycheck. And we start with a side hustle. But it doesn't have to stay that way—your side hustle can be your only hustle! It can be your life.

New rules. New games. I am so excited to see our generation redefining success on our own terms. I, too, have redefined my life. Consider *The Mocha Manual* your playbook. In it you'll find expert advice, inspiration, and successful strategies from other players in this game. Because like any black woman, when you play, you play to win! Game on.

CHAPTER ONE

Reclaim Your Passion and Purpose

I will never forget the moment it happened for me. I was sitting in my office at the New York City headquarters of *Essence* magazine, four floors above the hustle of midtown, enjoying what seemed to be, for any black female journalist, a dream job. I was a senior editor at *Essence,* the premier lifestyle magazine for black women. The phones were ringing, my assistant was overwhelmed, pages were due, designs needed to be done, and I was in the zone of doing what I do. In my job of managing the personal finance and careers department, I constantly read the anecdotes of inspiring women who took charge of their lives, their careers, and their finances. We featured these women every month to inspire our readers. And so I spent many fifteen-hour days crafting or editing stories about women who followed their passion, women who took a leap of faith, and women who had the courage to create a new life for themselves. Prior to joining *Essence,* I spent over a decade as a business journalist, most of that time writing for *Fortune* magazine, helping rich people get richer and writing profiles of the business world's success stories, from mostly-white captains of industry who created something small out of their garage and turned it into Microsoft or Google to mavericks at work who thought outside the box and transformed someone else's company. But never did I ask, What about me? Until the day I did. I stopped in the midst of the frenetic noise of closing an issue, and in a mental hush, I silently questioned myself. Did I want a life of writing about inspirational women or did I want to be one? Of course, I absolutely understand that having a senior position at such a magazine is an inspiration to many women. I've met many of them in my mentoring work. But there's a price I paid for being an office inspiration and not a living inspiration. For one, it became clear to me that my children spent more time with their sitter than they did with me. My marriage was crumbling. And I was sleep deprived from my own side hustle—the Mocha Manual Company. The online business was growing. I was filling orders until late at night, our events for moms had taken off and were being planned in cities across the country, and my mind was flooded with new ideas, next steps, and big plans.

I continued working at my great job with the appearance of a great life. But inside I wanted more. So on this day I decided there was a better life for me and my children beyond a high-profile job at a high-profile women's glossy and that I could choose to create that life for myself. Time had become my most precious asset, my role as a mother had become my primary identity, and I needed work that honored that. And then, in that instant, standing in the mental sanctum I created for myself in that frantic moment and teetering on the brink of a failed marriage and single motherhood, I took a deep breath and decided to transform my life.

I imagine the feeling I experienced at that moment to be much like when a trapeze artist, high in the big top after a few heart-pumping swings, actually releases the trapeze bar. Those few spectacular seconds when he's suspended in midair are the most amazing part of the act. With one bar fading into the background and the other coming toward him, it is at this moment when anything can happen. It is at this moment when there is no past, no future, only the present. This is when he defies gravity. This is when he flies. This is how I felt, hurling myself into the air, letting go of my trapeze. Up there, soaring, I saw a glimpse of how large my life could be.

Then came the gut-wrenching free-fall feeling—a pulse-racing sensation that was foreign to my secure and calculated direct-deposit-every-other-Thursday life. That feeling of uncertainty and insecurity was (and sometimes still is) completely uncomfortable, mostly because of the worry that I might fall and fail. But instead of resisting and fearing this uncertainty, on this day I decided to embrace it. On other occasions, I had allowed this fear of the unknown to send me running back to my comfy office. But on this day, I gave myself license to reinvent myself and, for once, not know the outcome. I was able to let go of my need to know and open my mind to taking the ride. There was something so exhilarating and liberating in that moment for me that it helped me later realize that the thrill of life is not in the landing—it's in the flying.

That very same day, on my hour-and-a-half train commute home, I began to map out an exit strategy from my job and to create a life plan that included time for children, financial independence, and work focused around the Mocha Manual and my passion—empowering black women as moms and moms-to-be. I was about to dive headfirst into a heart-opening adventure, and I felt like a million bucks.

If you're reading this book, most likely you've realized there's something better for you out there too. You want to create a life of financial freedom based on doing what you love on your own time instead of on a cycle of trading time for money in the nine-to-five world. You want to wake up every day with a smile and a zest for whatever possibilities the day will bring. You crave a life where your creativity and talents thrive without limits. You desire to be a part of an organization or a movement that embraces your core values. You want to fly! I understand you. I used to get up and go to work every day; now I get up every day and go to *life,* and let me tell you, ladies, it is the most incredible feeling.

You can do it too. This book is designed to help you get there. For many women the problem is not figuring out the *what,* it's figuring out the *how.* Most of us know where our passion lies. We know what we love doing. Research has proven that often, despite our own confusion and uncertainty, most people have pretty good instincts about what they should be doing with their lives. You've probably recognized this. The problem is that you're doing the thing you love on the weekends, after work, after the kids are asleep, and after everything else you have to do in life. The challenge is to reverse that pattern to make the passion your life.

The payoff is huge, but the road to be traveled is full of challenges. For starters, as you might expect, when you choose to create a life outside the usual boundaries of conventional ideas about work, folks begin to talk. The hateration starts spreading like gangrene. As I began to speak to those closest to me about my exit strategy, many people thought I was crazy to think about leaving *Essence* (and many still do to this day). At times even I thought I was crazy to leave such a "great" job and a six-figure salary. My daddy thought I was emotionally unstable and kept reminding me of my New York University and Columbia University education. Others began to ask, "Why today? Why not when . . ." (add your favorite future "someday scenario" here, including: when you have more money, when your youngest child starts school, when you are divorced, when the moons align, when you're forty years old, when we get our forty acres and a mule . . .). There were plenty of reasons to create that someday scenario. You know how we wait for the one illustrious day when somehow our finances, romantic relationship, personal values, spiritual state, and business skills are perfectly aligned with the constellations and everything in life is wonderfully and miraculously in place. Let me tell you, those days are hard to come by. In fact, I'd argue that they do not exist. Not one woman interviewed during the exhaustive research for this book has ever found that one day. The truth is, you can wait for that day or you can create your someday today. Instead of being subject to my circumstances, I decided to be the master of my circumstances, to make them fit with what I wanted from life.

This wasn't an easy move. And it was scary as hell. Like you, I had so many reasons to stay at the job and play it safe. Money. Health insurance. Two children. Money. (Did I say that already?) Mortgage. Car notes. Private school tuition. But sometimes it's the people who have the courage to ignore the reasons, those who are completely unreasonable in their thinking, who are the ones that ultimately create a life worth living.

Perhaps you too have plenty of "good reasons" for staying in your nine-to-five job. There could also be a host of circumstances in your life that make you feel that your passion should remain a side hustle while you spend the greater part of your waking hours doing work that does not fulfill you. And it is certainly risky to strike out on your own to build a moneymaking business that supports you and the lifestyle you want for yourself. Today, I will ask you to ignore those reasons. I will ask you to do something completely counterintuitive and let yourself stay in the uncomfortable place. Today I will ask you to focus on not what you get out of your workaday life, but what you *don't* get from it. How long can you stand by and let your dreams go unfulfilled? What daydream comes to you again and again that you keep pushing out of your mind? What are you waiting for? Consider what's lacking from your life that keeps you feeling unsatisfied and limited by what others say your worth is. Because for all the reasons why people continue in jobs they hate, the truth is, at your job, you'll never get paid what you're really worth. You will never have a life of complete fulfillment and a lifestyle of freedom, flexibility, and creativity that can only come from working for yourself. The life of entrepreneurship and following your passion is a lifestyle centered on connecting, birthing, and living the bigger dream, without compromise. It's the difference between designing your own life and being a slave to it. It's the difference between a life of "coulda," "woulda," "shoulda" and a life of true happiness. There's little true happiness in a life within safe walls. True happiness and genuine self-esteem grow from moving toward your desires and dreams. Happiness comes from the continual challenge to go beyond yourself as part of something greater than your own self-interest.

Don't just take my word for it. Now, I'm not the kind of sister who goes around quoting philosophical tidbits, especially from Hungarian-born cats with names I can't pronounce. But Mihaly Csikszentmihályi, a leading professor in positive psychology, sets it straight in his bestselling, groundbreaking book, *Flow: The Psychology of Optimal Experience,* when he writes:

> *Contrary to what we usually believe, the best moments in our lives are not the passive, receptive, relaxing times—although such experiences can also be enjoyable, if we worked hard to attain them. The best moments usually occur when a person's body or mind is stretched to its limits in a voluntary effort to accomplish something difficult or worthwhile.*

The idea of *flow* is just like being in the zone or in the groove and is defined as a state of intrinsic motivation, optimal fulfillment, and engagement, Csikszentmihályi argues. In an interview with *Wired* magazine, Csikszentmihályi described flow as "being completely involved in an activity for its own sake. The ego falls away. Time flies. Every action, movement, and thought follows inevitably from the previous one, like playing jazz. Your whole being is involved, and you're using your skills to the utmost." That feeling has been proven to lead to intense feelings of happiness, freedom, and fulfillment. Wouldn't you like a little of that in your life?

You don't have to be a college professor, a well-read individual, or Hungarian born, for that matter, to know these things. As you will see in this book, women just like you, from all walks of life, with all sorts of issues, baggage, and insecurities, and coming from various education levels and all sorts of life circumstances—some high school dropouts, some with children, sick parents to care for, past drug addictions, husbands, was-bands, and even baby daddy drama have learned this secret. They have put their lives in action, making things happen to master their circumstances and create a passion-centered life for themselves. You can too!

After all, the biggest factor in success typically has more to do with lacking fear than having anything else. Fear is the four-letter word that keeps countless women stuck in a rut and far away from the life of their dreams. Most of us are riddled with self-doubt and anxiety, both of which are energy-sapping emotions that don't do anything but impede creative forward movement. Can I really do this? Will I make any money? Do I have what it takes to make it happen? For many, the most important step is gaining confidence—finding your swagger—and a willingness to consider another perspective. Another life. We usually don't realize that it's usually our circumstances, our upbringing, and cultural messaging that have made us lose confidence. In reality, you have everything you need to move forward and create anything and everything you desire in your life. "When I learned to release the fear and have confidence in myself, that is when a new world of possibilities opened up for me," says Kristin St. James, who started a public relations firm in Richmond, Virginia, that now boasts over thirty paying clients.

With nothing holding you back, you are free to fully explore what you love to do. Discovering your passion is not necessarily a complex psychological analysis; it's more about reconnecting with your strengths. Our strengths are things that make us feel energized and alive—they give us a sense of accomplishment. We're not talking about just what we're good at; I've been trained to be good at financial calculations, but that doesn't make it my passion or something I want to spend the rest of my life doing. Your passion feeds your soul, gives you a sense of fulfillment like nothing else does. If you don't know what your passion is or what skill you can use to launch a successful business, we'll walk you through a few exercises in the next chapter that will help you find the right fit.

Right now, it's time for some cold hard facts. There's no way to sugarcoat this: entrepreneurship is risky. According to Dun and Bradstreet, the failure rate for new businesses seems to be 70 to 80 percent in the first year, and only about half of those that survive the first year will remain in business the next five years. Those numbers can be intimidating, but researchers are also very clear about the causes of business failure, and after reading this book you'll have minimized your chance of falling into one of the business-killing traps.

But even with great preparation and great inspiration, entrepreneurship is not for the faint of heart. You need serious emotional endurance to stick at something day in, day out, continuously being self-motivated even when things are not going well. You need to be bullheaded and unwilling to accept the status quo, and have a high energy level, a strong passion, and an ability to create a clear vision for how something should be.

To get all that going you may need to retrain your brain. Specifically, try to redefine your ideas about risk. Sure, starting a business involves a good measure of risk. But consider the mental, emotional, and physical costs of working in an environment that isn't suited to you—that may be the greatest danger of all. Looking back on a life of "coulda been," and "what ifs" is even more risky for your happiness and sense of self. People who work for themselves are more fulfilled because regardless of their level of success they are building something important; they are crafting from a passion. Even the business owner who is working eighteen-hour days, hasn't broken even yet, or can't go out to dinner with friends as often as she'd like is still significantly more fulfilled than her corporate sister.

So now ask yourself, what about me? Why not me?

Here's what you need to begin this journey. For you to successfully create a passion-centered life, you have to:

1. **Embrace the uncertainty.** Learn to let go of your need to know. View life with curiosity and a sense of adventure instead of with fear and anxiety.

2. **Be adaptable.** Things happen. Plans fall apart. "It's not the strongest species that survives, it's not even the most intelligent, it is the one most responsive to change," goes a quote attributed to Charles Darwin. When circumstances change, be they personal, financial, or in your industry (and trust me, they will), be willing to readjust your plan.

3. **Have boundless energy.** This ain't easy. Don't think that entrepreneurship is a life of leisurely lunches and sleeping in. You will likely work harder than you ever have in your life, especially in the early days. You need energy and devotion to make it work. Energy will help you get your business up and running, and good stamina will keep it afloat. Without endurance, no business can succeed.

4. **Be resourceful.** Can you make a dollar out of fifteen cents? Ever made a satisfying dinner out of damn near nothing in the fridge? Well, business success also comes from drawing on all your resources, thinking outside the box, and being willing to use your know-how and network to make something out of nothing.

5. **Have amazing networking skills.** Are you a natural connector? No man (or woman) is an island, especially if she is building a business. You will need to meet others, get customers, make industry contacts, and more to make your business grow.

6. **Realize that the only thing stopping you is you!** When you think big and dream big and follow through with sacrifice and dogged determination, there is nothing you can't accomplish. Just get out of your own way, put aside your insecurities and that little voice in your head that says you can't, and go make it happen!

Mocha Mix
How I Rediscovered My Passion

* * * * * * * * * * * * * * * *

If you want to turn your passion into profit, write down your vision and surround yourself with people of skill, expertise, and wisdom who can help you work your plan. I knew I had the gift to lead. When I finally recognized my strengths, then all of my prayers and lifestyle choices began to focus on how I could move in that direction. After that, I started to do health care consulting and I loved it! I decided to apply my strengths to that industry and start my own rehabilitation company.
— SHARON SAULS, CEO of SKY Neurological Rehabilitation, a full-service outpatient rehab center in Maryland (www.skyneurorehab.com)

I figured out early on that my mission was to remember why I'm here on this earth. What problems am I here to solve? For me, that meant looking at the intersection of my gifts and talents and what goods or service I could provide.
— KAREN TAYLOR BASS, president and CEO of Taylor Made Media, a professional empowerment agency in New York (www.taylormademediapr.com)

I remember annoying the hell out of my husband with my need to organize, my love affair with a label maker, and my fascination with color-coded systems. I used to

beat myself up about my obsession, and then I realized that it was a skill that unorganized people would pay for. I get such joy out of restoring order to a room or closet. I feel so good after conquering chaos. I know it's a weird passion. But I finally figured out how to not view it as a problem and accept it as a passion that can pay.
— Sheila Johnston, owner of OrganizeThis, an organizational and design service in Atlanta

I have always loved everything related to looking good and feeling good, so it was a natural fit for me to open a nail salon but provide a better experience for clients.
— Tricialee Riley, owner of Polish Bar of Brooklyn, New York, an upscale nail salon (www.polishbar brooklyn.com)

Just look at what you do well, focus on your strengths in any area, and develop them into something you enjoy doing or something you always wanted to do. Understand your weaknesses so you can work around them.
— Shaquanda Spivey, president of SOLUTIONS Drug Testing Services, LLC, a drug testing service in New Jersey (www.solutionsdts.com)

When you see your passion and business venture come together, it feels like that moment in a movie where you hear chimes in the background and see a light. Everything becomes clear and you see how and why certain things happened in your past . . . to lead you to the steps you are at now.

— MIA SEARS, CEO of Posh VIP Ltd., an entertainment, event planning, and publicity company in Cincinnati, Ohio (www.posh-vip.com)

I was nineteen, lying in the grass in the park with a good friend, discussing life, when I realized that the world was available to me . . . I was the only person holding me back. I didn't know it then, but that realization and developing that kind of mind-set was good preparation for stepping into entrepreneurship years later.

— MARSHA BURNETT, president of Musical Directions, of New York/Detroit/Los Angeles/London, which provides tour production and management to a client roster that includes Beyoncé, Faith Evans, Stevie Wonder, and Mary J. Blige (www.musicaldirections .com)

FROM THE STREETS TO SATIN

Doreen Motton, president and CEO of Neero & Ana, creator of
the Satin Slumber Collection (www.neero-ana.com)

Doreen Motton has the ultimate motivator: "Every time I want to get down on myself, I remember living in my car, living in a bottle, and losing my son to the system. God didn't bring me all this way for me to give up now," she says.

Doreen's journey up the ranks to Citigroup vice president and then taking the entrepreneur plunge at age fifty included one major obstacle: herself. "I was always told I was never going to be anything, but deep down I knew I was destined to be something else. I always wanted to be bigger than I was. And I knew I had something to offer. But in the back of my head I was struggling with who I was and who I wanted to be," she says.

What she did know is that whatever insecurities she had disappeared when she had a drink in her hand.

A "functional addict" for years, Doreen always had a job and even a few side hustles. After graduating from Northeastern, she worked for Dun and Bradstreet, a financial research firm, for several years. During that time, her boyfriend's father was a distributor for Seagram and her side hustle was to get patrons to try it and get stores and bars to buy more of the product. "It was a promotion business called Liquid Assets and I hired some people who would organize and sponsor happy hours. But I was always too wasted to hold a meeting or get the staff together, so it fell apart within a year. I had lost my credibility and people didn't trust me. But, you know what, I had my own demons, and they were my friends."

Doreen transformed her life struggles into a formula for perseverance and success in her business. She shares these hard-earned lessons with you:

Face the truth about your life

For ten years I was on a descent into the devil's lounge. There was a time when I lived in my car and looked for love in all the wrong places. I was wasting my life with something either up my nose or in my hand. I'm not proud of that but I always knew there was an angel with me. I survived what others didn't.

If there are any women reading this who are struggling within themselves, I'm here to tell you that there's a way out of the way you think and how you live. I made a conscious decision to do something about my life and how I viewed myself. And then every day I lived it! One day at a time.

Recognize your gifts

I knew I was on a quest to find myself and use the talents God gave me, but I had been suppressing it. I wanted to be an entrepreneur. I always had a fondness for people and building friendships. I liked sales and marketing. There was something about the power of persuasion that I thought I did well.

When life is trying to tell you something . . . listen

There was a series of events over time that changed my life. I always had the same hairdresser for fifteen years. I loved what she did with my hair, and when I would ask how to keep this look so fabulous, she always asked, "Did you get your satin pillowcase? Your ends are busted; your hair is dry . . ." When I finally found one it would fade after a few months of washing. Then it hit me: I could make my own. So I did.

A little while later I was unemployed. I made a few of my satin pillowcases, monogrammed them, and gave them away as Christmas gifts. Everyone loved them. Then one day I was on my way home from the salon and the idea about the satin pillowcases as an actual business came to me in a voice. I knew they worked for me, I knew others liked them, and I could use my experience and talents. I was open and receptive to the message.

When my fiftieth birthday came, it was a real epiphany for me. I realized that I had more years behind me than ahead of me, so whatever I was going to do I needed to do it now.

Get your tools of the trade

I went to Staples and got the business card kit and I made the cards myself. I knew that would be an affirmation. As a smoker, if I had matches, I knew I could stop smoking, but if I had a lighter I was definitely a smoker—that is the tool for smoking. I wanted to have a card and give that out and validate who I was. I wanted the tools for being in business.

Give it your all

Every waking and sleeping moment I thought about these satin pillowcases: How will I make them? What kind of fabric? How will I package it? I did all the research myself. I attended fabric shows to find the right satin. Then I went from a plain pillowcase to adding branding and embellishments.

Research relentlessly

Take advantage of all the free resources to research, research, and research. When you have the passion, the exploration comes easy.

Start small

In 2004 I saw a sign for a sewing machine sale and I went there and bought a sewing machine. At night when I came home from Citigroup, I would sew. I could only make one an hour. Then I hired others to sew for me, but relying on people to deliver with the same quality that I wanted didn't really work. I started researching manufacturers.

Then I started small, selling within organizations, to friends and family, and going to local black expos and other vending events.

Seize the moment

One day as I was driving in to work, I heard Karen Taylor Bass of Taylor Made Media on our local radio station; she was talking about how entrepreneurs can get themselves out there. Before I even got my coffee I called her. We began to work together and she helped me tremendously—she did a series of press releases and helped with my branding, marketing collateral, and advertising. Karen told me about an upcoming story in *Ebony* magazine about women in corporate America with other side businesses, and I was included in the story.

Be ready for success

After the *Ebony* story, sales hit the roof in December and January of 2007. In February 2007, I decided that I didn't want this to be a side hustle anymore. I came alive at 6:00 P.M. when I left Citigroup. I was stressed at my day job. There was a hiring freeze, people were being laid off, and that meant more work for me. I had to be there late and in early, which interfered with my time to run my business, and I hated who I had become. I was exhausted. On February 13 my boss pissed me off for the last time and I decided to quit. That happened on a Tuesday; I was out of there on Friday. I felt a tremendous sense of relief. I'm not a spring chicken—I should have been thinking about retirement and not about giving up benefits, wonderful perks, and job security. But I knew I would be okay.

Don't let doubt take root

For a fleeting moment, I questioned myself, but literally within thirty minutes the cell phone rang and I got a call from the NAACP Image Awards asking me to be a part of the celebrity gift bag suite. They saw my product in the *Ebony* magazine article. It was a confirmation that I was going to be okay. I've been on a rampage ever since.

Have a higher purpose

My business is a conduit for me to touch someone else's life. This is a smokescreen so I can meet people, share my story, and effect change. In order for me to benefit from everything that I've learned, I've got to give it away—and giving it away is sharing some wisdom. That's my calling and that is where I need to be. Through my work, I reach out to group homes, victims of domestic violence, and breast cancer patients.

Persevere no matter what

Make sure you really have a passion for this. A lot of people will say, "I tried this but this didn't work out, then I tried this." You can't keep doing that. You have to keep listening to the voice inside that's guiding you and know that this was meant for you to do. It's like a real baby. You can't ditch the baby because you're tired or it cries too much.

Don't be stopped by failures

Failures? Oh, hell yes I've had them! The first summer after I left Citigroup it was one of the most difficult summers I ever had. After a through-the-roof winter, sales were in a slump. I realized I was thinking too much about this moment when there were few sales. And I'm stinking because I'm thinking. Instead of thinking about low sales, I think about other avenues to market myself and ask myself who else needs to know about me. I get on the Internet, Google a few things, send out a media kit—anything to get in action and moving forward.

Claim your victory

I have been sober for over ten years and counting. That confirms for me that I can do or be anything!

CHAPTER TWO

Fit Matters: How to Find the Perfect Business Match

The future belongs to those who believe
in the beauty of their dreams.
—*Eleanor Roosevelt*

Life is not about finding yourself, it's
about creating yourself.
—*George Bernard Shaw*

Everybody is good at something. Everyone has an innate talent and gift. This is what I know. It's the way God made us. And not just humans, it's the way God made the animals too. Think about it: every species in nature has everything it needs to survive. There is no living thing that isn't inherently equipped with the skills and abilities it needs to secure its continued existence. Even Earth has every cycle, from evaporation and condensation to photosynthesis, to sustain itself and all the life forms on it. Whether it's through instinct, size, camouflage, or speed, no lion or giraffe has ever had to go to trade school to learn what it needs to know to survive.

In the same manner, every one of us has something we can use to ensure our own survival—a skill, a talent, or a personality trait that can be maximized into a tool to ensure our financial and business survival. In order to start a business that will beat the odds of failure and low earnings, you have to figure out what that is. Whether it's making cakes, making marketing campaigns, making computer software solutions, or making people laugh, every woman has something she is good at and enjoys doing that she can do to make money. Your first clue to finding a possible business venture is finding something at which you excel. But it must also be something you really enjoy doing. Want to live a fulfilled life? It's simple: do what you love. The thought of getting rich quick (or slowly!) may be appealing, but if you don't enjoy the work it will make for a very, very unhappy venture.

Sometimes your best asset is your creativity or a great idea. A great idea can just happen; other times discovering our talents and skills requires a deeper look. My creative unfolding went like this: I had an idea to create a Mocha Manual maternity T-shirt for the purpose of promoting the pregnancy guidebook I wrote. I decided to have some shirts with our glamorous cover girl made as giveaways for various book events across the country. Women really liked the shirts! That early success was my inspiration to think bigger. Would people be willing to pay for these shirts? At my next event, I raffled one away but I also had five others to sell. I sold all five. The feeling was exhilarating. Was I onto something? Whether it's the first repeat client or selling out your first product line, it's a really good feeling to know that you're doing something right.

I had found a niche. The more I researched, the more I realized that there was very little merchandise for pregnant black women and their babies. And as I sold more shirts, I realized that I had the personality and know-how to market and sell T-shirts. After thirteen years as a business journalist, writing countless stories advising entrepreneurs on how to build solid companies or profiling moneymaking entrepreneurs, I had finally found the outlet for my knowledge and my passion for motherhood.

If you don't have a brilliant, patent-worthy idea, no worries. You don't have to reinvent the wheel to have a kick-butt business venture; sometimes you just have to improve on something that's already out there. Most successful businesses are born out of not innovation but necessity. Instead of trying to come up with an idea that changes the world, simply take a look at your world and see where there may be a void that needs filling or a business concept that needs improvement. Scores of moms have started million-dollar businesses by simply creating or improving on a product. Let's face it, Domino's Pizza was certainly not the first to offer home delivery of pizza, but it was the first to guarantee it would be delivered piping hot to your door in thirty minutes or less. Amazon.com was not the first company to sell books, but it was one of the first that would let you buy books from the comfort of your own home while sitting in your robe.

Whether you are led by a talent, a great idea, or an improvement on an existing product or service, every successful sister entrepreneur is, first of all, very clear about who she is and what she's good at. You may be talented at making jewelry but may not have the discipline to fulfill orders or the desire to deal with customers. That could mean that it may be better to sell your jewelry to another company that will sell it and deal with the customer service hassles for you. Maybe you can earn money by licensing your designs to a company. Either way, there's more than one way to skin a cat. And there's more than one way to make an idea pay off. It is better to have the *type* of business that suits your personality and skills than to let your passion/talent alone dictate a business direction that then becomes unsustainable. Should you offer a product or a service? Should you look into direct sales or network marketing?

Some women may even consider purchasing a franchise or an already established business. The idea of starting something from scratch may be unappealing. Investing money in a turnkey operation that has gone through the start-up hiccups can be an attractive option if you do your research properly (read chapter 6 for more on franchising or buying an existing business). Opening a franchise or buying a business has its own required skill set. So before you can fully explore any of these options, let's start with a little self-exploration.

Know Thyself, Find Thyself

Entrepreneurship is more than a business maneuver; it's a mind game that starts with a deep self-awareness and ends with self-determination. The self-awareness helps you understand your personality type, identify your passions and aptitudes, and connect the two with a good business fit. When you can get all three of those factors properly aligned, you can greatly improve your chances of business success. Of course, there will always be necessary business skills to learn (which we'll address in chapter 5), but when the business fundamentally blends with your personality type, any gaps in skills can be addressed via your business team and support network. It is a lot easier to bring in someone with marketing know-how than to teach someone how to be a people person. So you need to be honest with yourself about your strengths and weaknesses, flaws and foibles, things you excel at and things that, well, not so much. Take time to ask close friends and loved ones about aspects of your personality they have observed—sometimes the way we perceive ourselves is *way* different from the way others see us.

Remember the Time

One of the first places to look for clues to your true calling and perfect-fit business venture is the mirror. It's time to go way back and get to know yourself. Not getting to know yourself as in you've been a stranger all these years, but more like reconnecting with your former self. Remember the self you were before you were stressed out, before the kids, before you became a slave to your mortgage, before you were cynical, complacent, apathetic, dreamless, or any combination thereof. Remember the you from when you dared to dream big, saw your life as limitless, and saw yourself as invincible. By doing so, you will most certainly find your calling—what you are here to do. Your passion in life comes from your interests; it emanates from what stimulates you and really gets a fire going under your bottom.

To get more clarity on this passion-finding business, I set about talking to various business coaches, experts, gurus, and hurus about how you find your passion. Is a trancelike state required? Heck, does everyone even have an all-consuming passion? Is a passionless existence possible, even probable, and can a woman be a successful business owner without the passion quotient?

To begin my fact-finding mission, I had an empowering conversation with a man named Andrew Morrison, who runs a successful small-business boot camp (www.90dayplan.com) to help coach entrepreneurs but admits he spends more time coaching them through the emotional healing required for business success than the rudiments of business ownership. For the past eighteen years, Morrison has been a successful serial entrepreneur. He built a multimillion-dollar business from scratch by providing direct marketing services to *Fortune* 500 companies. For his accomplishment, he was featured on Oprah's show on young millionaires. Working primarily with black women, Morrison has literally helped thousands of entrepreneurs find their true calling and use it to reach phenomenal financial success and new levels of personal growth. His advice to help women identify their calling is this: "I don't advise people to *find* their calling, I tell them to *remember* their calling. Wake up to it. Wake up to your greatness." Andrew's first question to most new clients is a pretty startling one. "Who convinced you out of your calling? Who told you that you could not be bold and beautiful?" he says. "This event usually occurred in childhood—a time when you told yourself you couldn't do something. Your mission is to remember why you were sent to Earth. What problem are you here to solve? Ask your friends and family. What do you do naturally that you don't see as a gift? Your calling is not something you have to find."

Face Value

Andrea Fairweather, the thirty-eight-year old owner of Fairweather Faces, the hugely successful mobile makeup and spa service (www.fairweatherfaces.com), only had to look down to remember her calling. "Since the age of eight to ten years old I took my hands very seriously. I had photo-shoot-ready nails every day. I was excited by the colors. When I was in high school, my nails matched my outfits every day. And not just one color; I had four or five colors that blended perfectly. And I could paint on a dime, so I would do nail art for my girlfriends like writing their boyfriends' names on their nails," Andrea says. Now that's a passion.

Years went by, with Andrea loving her nails and her father reminding her that her studies were the priority—not polish. Andrea later went to the State University of New York and majored in dance, another lifelong interest. But one day, while admittedly trying to show off in dance class, she leaped into the air and landed badly, sustaining a sprain that would severely compromise her ability to pursue dance full-time over the long term.

This was a life-changing moment for Andrea. She was depressed by the not-knowing-ness of seeing her life's plans dashed in front of her. But prior to the fall, she had slowly been realizing that the life of a dancer was not really what she thought it would be. "I was burned out physically and mentally from the dance but I didn't know how to walk away from it," she says. Slowly, she began to remember her calling. In fact, it had never left her life. Even at college, she was always the one who got calls to do hair and nails on campus. She had booked appointments and purchased supplies. But Andrea still never saw it as anything but a side hustle. In her final semester, she says her spirit kept drawing her to take a business course. She couldn't figure out why. But she decided to listen to her spirit anyway. As a final project in that college class, Andrea had to create a business plan. The concept she submitted became the preliminary blueprint for Fairweather Faces—a full-service salon that comes to your home or office.

Ten years later, Fairweather Faces operates in eight major metropolitan areas and consistently earns more than half a million dollars in annual sales. From New York to Los Angeles,

Andrea's celebrity roster is extensive. And she has her father's full support—he even helped out as a driver in the early days, making sure the nail and makeup artists got to their appointments on time. Not bad for a girl hooked on nail polish. Even now, she has a full closet dedicated exclusively to her extensive collection of nail colors. But she also has a sizable bank account!

One of the many great lessons of Andrea's story is that she never forgot the thing that made her happy, the thing she loved so much she did it for free, and even though she had other interests and skills, she never forgot what got her excited every day. And when her spirit began leading her toward something, she listened. What is your spirit leading you to?

SELF-ASSESSMENT

- **Ask yourself:**
- **What are you doing when you feel happiest?**
- **What do you love about yourself?**
- **Think back to your childhood: What did you want to be before fear and cynicism set in?**
- **If money were no object, what would you want to do?**
- **Allow yourself the luxury of daydreaming; what do you think about doing?**
- **What is the one thing other people say you're good at?**
- **List five things you really enjoy doing and five things you're really good at.**

When you realize that your passion is not something you have to find but something you already know, the possibilities are limitless. And the task doesn't seem so daunting. It's simply a matter of reconnecting with your past.

Robin Wilson went back four generations to find her dream

business. "Real estate is in my blood," she once said in a magazine interview. Her grandfather owned several Texas "shotgun" houses—studios where oil workers lived. As a young girl she would spend time with her grandfather caring for the properties. When she was seven years old, Wilson says, her grandfather let her choose the exterior paint colors. She made one block the "rainbow" houses, with one blue, one violet, one red, and so on. "It made caring for property seem like art. On Sundays we collected rent. That made real estate seem like an ATM—you can get money out of it," she said.

Years later, Robin took a more winding path to her passion. After college, she went into management consulting, then executive recruitment. But she was frustrated that she would only find people jobs and never knew whether it was actually a good match or not. It was as if she started projects but didn't finish them. In 1999, her firm went public and she sold her shares to go to graduate school and study real estate finance.

Even then she was still trying to find her way. She met closed door after closed door in commercial property management and had little interest in becoming a broker. Then a professor suggested residential property management, and she thought that would be more like what her grandfather did. To start, she convinced friends to let her manage the renovation of their kitchens, bathrooms, or baby rooms. She came in and managed the whole project from start to finish, leaving the homeowner worry free. Then she did whole apartments and offices.

Now, her company, Robin Wilson Home, manages renovation budgets as high as $7 million. Wilson managed the renovation of former president Clinton's office in Harlem and the renovation of the Mélange salon at the swanky Peninsula hotel in New York City. She enjoys design management and continues the family history of real-estate-related enterprises. Business is booming.

There are other places besides your past to find clues to your passion, too. Some of them are in the most unlikely of places.

Passion in Your Job?

At times we look for our passion and our strengths outside of our daily life or even outside of our nine-to-five job, as if our passion were an escape from our everyday life. Or we think it has to be the opposite of what we presently do every day. Sometimes it is. And sometimes it isn't. When you really think about your day job, there are likely aspects of it that you really enjoy. Maybe it's your boss who drives you to drink or the administrative tasks that bore you into a narcoleptic fit, but there are likely responsibilities that you savor—meeting with clients, presenting big ideas, preparing reports, planning events, and so on. Perhaps somewhere among the aspects of your day job that you like, you can also find the kind of business that would best suit your personality and the types of activities that you would enjoy doing on a daily basis. So before you fire your boss, see what you can learn about yourself from your job.

Start a work journal. Spend a few weeks writing down what you like and what you don't like about your job. Be as specific as possible, itemizing exactly what you were doing during the times of day when you felt alive as well as the times you felt miserable.

At the age of thirty, Jennifer Thompson followed this same exercise. She had grown tired of her job as an account manager for an advertising agency and was fairly convinced that she hated everything about the job. Instead, through this exercise she realized that, like many of us, she had lumped the overriding feeling of misery about her job into the whole job, when there were actually parts of the job that fit well with her strengths and passions. As Jennifer began keeping her work journal, she realized that she felt great when she was interacting with people. Jennifer didn't necessarily see her love for engagement with people as a strength to be analyzed and considered when choosing her entrepreneurial venture. But it was. She also experienced a joyous adrenaline rush when presenting in front of small groups, and even enjoyed the frenzied pace of the pre-presentation prep work. She hated the administrative tasks and found that she struggled to follow up on small details. After keeping a work journal and working with a business coach, Jennifer launched a marketing consulting firm. That allowed her to capitalize on her strong presentation, big-picture thinking, and people skills; secure clients; develop an overall strategy; and then delegate the execution. It was a perfect fit and something she would not have considered without carefully analyzing her present job requirements. Sometimes, we just have to pull apart the layers of our daily existence. You may also find that examining your job can give you clues to finding your passion and the right business fit. There may be something else lurking in your workplace.

Look for business leads. When you're doing something every day you have the best perspective on what works about the process and what doesn't. How many times have you said, "We really need this product or software," or "I wish someone offered this service?" Well, that someone could be you and your business. Do you see a need for goods or services that is presently unmet or can you think of a better way to do something? If so, you might have the seed for a profitable business.

By improving upon a current idea (remember Domino's Pizza) you can step right into a profitable business with a proven success record by simply providing something faster, better, or more economically. Think about it.

> **Tough Times Tip:** Even in an economic downturn, there may be a blessing in disguise at your workplace. Many enterprising women have turned a company layoff, restructuring, or downsizing into the perfect opportunity to start their own thing. If there is talk of layoffs or cutbacks at your job, don't panic. Consider if this may be an opportunity to pursue your business plans. Read this book faster to start working on your business skills and transition plan. You may even want to anonymously inquire if you can volunteer for a buyout.

Next Steps

Now, take a look at your lists. First look at the things you enjoy or enjoyed doing. Whether they are from childhood or from your current job, start looking at these ideas as possible businesses. Sometimes your strengths and interests are directly linked to a business idea, like making jewelry or doing graphic design. Or your passion may be to inspire others or to educate. In those instances, the actual business idea may not be so clear-cut. Either way, you must find the value in your passion. Is there a product or service related to this interest that you could market and sell? If you have a passion for food, you could start your own restaurant or license your secret recipe to a restaurant. How do you know which business type is best for you? Keep reading! Someone who is detail-oriented could be a professional researcher or organizer. If you enjoy motivating and inspiring others, learn how you can make money as a motivational speaker. If your happiest moments are when you are working with children, how can you market services related to children, from child care to party entertainment? Be willing to look at your calling from 360 degrees. Research on the Internet and in business publications to see if someone else is making money by doing what you aspire to do. Ask yourself, "Is there information about my passion that people want to know? Is there a book, video, DVD, website, lecture, or workshop I can offer to share what I know about my passion?" Ask your close friends and relatives if they know of anyone doing that or something related to your dream. Can your passion be used to guide, teach, or direct others to achieve goals they desire? Remember, whatever has value for you will automatically have value for others. Through speaking about your passion comes the confirmation that it is real, viable, and possible. Within the questioning lies answers.

What's Your Personality Type?

As you're thinking about what type of business would work best for your passion and interests, it's equally important to make sure this business suits your personality too. You may be passionate about motivating others. But if you're too shy to speak in front of large audiences, then motivational speaking may not be the best fit. Are you a go-getter who likes to interact with customers or would you rather work behind the scenes? Do you need to be running the show or are you more of a team player? Understanding your personality type is the next step in making sure your path of passion can lead to business success. Several studies indicate that successful entrepreneurs share a number of personality traits and that these traits can often determine how successful you will be as an entrepreneur. Research suggests that these personality qualities are more important than education, skills, and experience in determining who makes it as a successful business owner and who doesn't. The key to success is selection. So this is important stuff. Everyone has the potential to grow a business successfully when they are coupled with the right opportunity—one that suits their personality and comes from their calling. When you can really understand your personality, you can bridge the gap between what you are and what skills are required for your business. Then you can begin building the right team.

There's a lot of research out there about entrepreneurs and personality types. I like some of the work of a California-based behavioral consultancy, Accord Management Systems, which compiled their results after studying more than 1,500 entrepreneurs with sales of more than $1 million a year. Not bad. As a result they've figured out what makes some entrepreneurs wildly successful, what makes others moderately successful, and why others fail. With this in mind, entrepreneurs can figure out what they have and what they are lacking so they can improve their chances of success. Here's what these guys found: In general, successful entrepreneurs are often natural leaders and strong problem solvers. Overall, entrepreneurs come in two basic flavors: generalists and specialists—these two are pretty much polar opposites. As you read through this portion, think deeply about your personality and where you fit. Better yet, ask a friend for her assessment of your personality to make sure you're on target. Remember, selecting the right business fit is critical to success.

For the most part, this study found that generalists are strategic thinkers. They are big-picture oriented, prefer environments where they can use their results-driven nature, enjoy autonomy and independence, and are stronger risk takers. Specialists are tactical, prefer being responsible for areas within their expertise, are more detail oriented, and prefer environments that provide both security and stability. Specialists are typically more risk averse, unless they are working within their area of expertise.

Within the generalist and specialist types are four personality factors: dominance, sociability, relaxation, and compliance. Most personalities include these factors, whose respective opposites are acceptance, analytical, drive, and independence, to some degree.

Generalist personalities have a dominance factor that is greater than their compliance factor. Generalists are also known for their strong need to win and their belief that they are always right. If this is starting to sound like you, don't despair—it can be a good thing.

Specialist personalities are more compliant than dominant. They thrive by doing things by the book—following rules and procedures. They will try to do everything right, which usually means avoiding risks.

With that in mind, here are the seven broad personality types, according to Accord Management's research results. You can get a complimentary personality evaluation from Accord by calling 805-230-2100. For now, read on and see where you fit in.

The Trailblazer (I'm thinking Robin Givens as Jacqueline in the movie *Boomerang*)

IF YOU'RE A TRAILBLAZER

You are very competitive, ambitious, and goal oriented—so much so that you tend to be aggressive and sometimes take a steamroller approach. You're restless and energetic, with a strong drive and a sense of urgency, regardless of the task at hand. You tend to have two speeds: fast and faster. Independent, persistent, and decisive, you aren't happy unless you're in charge. Trailblazers are logical, analytical, practical, and realistic—you tend to base decisions on facts rather than feelings. You are a calculated risk taker.

The Trailblazer's Business Strengths

You can thrive in the medical, technology, finance, legal, and consulting fields. Your strong strategic thinking skills make you perfectly suited to focusing on operations and marketing. Your challenge is likely to be working with people—you are usually a better leader than manager and need to surround yourself with others who can manage the people side of the business. Trailblazers prefer being the driving force of a business. You typically wouldn't buy a franchise or distributorship, but you would start a company that competes with a franchise. You are highly innovative, especially when it comes to taking an idea to the next level.

The Go-Getter (I'm thinking Oprah!)

IF YOU'RE A GO-GETTER

You have a higher-than-average level of both dominance and sociability and are very driven and independent. You are competitive, but your drive to succeed is sometimes tempered by your interest in and concern for others. Accord's research revealed that Go-Getters represent the largest percentage of business founders. The natural style of go-getters lends itself to managing and leading both processes and people.

You show a great deal of initiative, coupled with a compelling sense of urgency to get things done. Go-Getters are typically good leaders and good managers, easily motivating themselves and those around them.

The Go-Getter's Business Strengths

You can do well in retail but may prefer being the outside rainmaker. You work well in ambitious and unfamiliar environments. This means you can invest in, buy, or start a business that's totally new to you and still make a success of it. You don't need to be an expert in the field to start the business—you are a good collaborator and can learn as you go.

The Manager (I'm thinking Nicole Ari Parker as Teri in the *Soul Food* television series)

IF YOU'RE A MANAGER

You are dominant and independent. In your case, these two characteristics feed each other, so you can appear to be even more dominant or independent than you actually are. You are also very goal-oriented and can be quite analytical, focusing more on processes and outcomes than on people. You have a tendency to look at people as vehicles for helping you accomplish your goals. Consequently, you sometimes disregard or overlook the people part of the equation or unwittingly offend people with your straightforward style of communication.

Unlike the two previous entrepreneurial types, Managers have a higher-than-average level of relaxation and know that some projects simply take more time to complete and some goals take longer to achieve than others. You're loyal, sometimes to a fault, as you consider your employees to be an extension of your family. You can deal well with customers, especially repeat customers, so you'll probably be great at growing a business.

The Manager's Business Strengths

You like doing things on your own, are a great behind-the-scenes leader, and love working with systems, concepts, ideas, and technologies. You excel at competitive selling because you enjoy overcoming rejection and achieving goals despite obstacles. Managers enjoy working by themselves, and managing others can be a challenge, so you need to hire employees who are better than you at listening and working well with others.

The Motivator (I'm thinking Susan Taylor, author, fourth-generation entrepreneur and the driving force behind building *Essence* magazine)

IF YOU'RE A MOTIVATOR

You have a high level of sociability, an above-average level of dominance, and are both driven and independent. This gives you the ability to work well under pressure and in autonomous situations. It also means that you will be a great consensus builder, a good collaborator, and a driver of change. Just like the name suggests, you are the consummate motivator who does well working by, with, and through others.

The Motivator's Business Strengths

Retail can be your game—or any environment where people are a large part of the equation. You do well in almost any business that involves people, as long as it's a somewhat nonconfrontational environment. You can be convincing and avoid most confrontation by creating a strong emotional argument. Motivators do well in the toughest of customer service roles, as you are able to see both sides of the argument. You tend to deal with even the most negative arguments by using the three F's—feel, felt, and found—saying, "I understand how you are feeling. In fact, I have felt the same way, but when I learned [insert your point], what I found was [again, insert your point]."

Motivators excel at leadership and sales. You do well in business with partners or in a business that involves others. Motivators are good at nurturing relationships and often do best in a business that involves keeping clients for the long term. You thrive in a team environment.

The Specialist Personalities

The Authority (I'm thinking Kimberly Elise as Helen in Tyler Perry's movie *Diary of a Mad Black Woman*)

IF YOU'RE AN AUTHORITY

You are the backbone of our society. Authorities are the loyal workers who make our world function—you make our products, service our systems, and always do it right. As an Authority, you may not always be the best founder of an entrepreneurial enterprise, but you can be an excellent distributor, franchisee, or owner of an existing business—you can do well when you purchase an ongoing operation.

You are detail and tactic oriented and are motivated by doing things one way—the right way. You are very conscientious and cooperative, following rules, procedures, and policies carefully. Very thorough with details, you're cautious, deliberate, logical, and analytical. You're also relaxed, patient, and accommodating by nature and are a great team player who tends to avoid confrontation. Examples of businesses that fit this personality type would be dry cleaning stores and liquor or convenience stores, where the need for the product or service is strong. You grow your customer base, embracing it with loyalty—you see your customers as an extension of your family.

The Authority's Business Strengths

Authorities often refer to themselves as "accidental" entrepreneurs, because they may end up running a business that was never part of their original plan. Consequently, you're best served by going into a business that embraces your level of expertise or allows you to develop a new level of expertise. Because you are accommodating, you may dislike prospecting, so you may need to be in a business where customers or clients seek you out. Most Authority types need a partner with a stronger natural ability to prospect and network. You can be very successful buying a franchise or business opportunity as long as the organization is well supported with advertising and marketing.

The Collaborator (I'm thinking Vanessa Williams as Maxine in the *Soul Food* television series)

IF YOU'RE A COLLABORATOR

The primary difference between you and Authorities is that you have a personality gift called sociability. It's this characteristic that allows you to use your influence to get what you want. It's all about people—you relish the people side of business.

You typically benefit from having a partner who is more aggressive about developing new business. Collaborators usually aren't comfortable with cold-calling or pitching new ideas; you like to follow prescribed rules and guidelines.

The Collaborator's Business Strengths

You're good at running customer-service-oriented or retail businesses, or any business where being convincing is an important aspect of getting the job done and done right. From an entrepreneurial perspective, Collaborators do well within structured environments where people are an element of success.

Collaborators can be great salespeople in a warm selling market because they use their sociability to sell their expertise. Warm selling means you bring the prospect to you, often through a letter or advertisement enticing the prospect to contact you for more information about your product or service. Once prospects do get in touch, your expertise takes over, and you sell your heart out. On the other hand, cold selling, which Generalist personalities typically do well, involves picking up the phone and dialing for dollars, or hitting the streets looking for prospects door-to-door.

The Diplomat (I'm thinking Tracee Ellis Ross as Joan on the television series *Girlfriends*)

IF YOU'RE A DIPLOMAT

You are restless and enjoy working under a certain amount of pressure. You get things done quickly and work well with deadlines. You adjust easily to change and deal well with new situations. You have a high sense of urgency and like variety, and because of your compliance and your need to do things right, you work at your full capacity. You multitask and keep a variety of jobs going at once. Active and energetic, you vigorously attack the parts of your business that you enjoy. You can experience difficulty in delegating details but do a great job when you can do the work yourself.

Diplomats are considered by many to be the best of the Specialist entrepreneurs, as they have both sociability and drive in their personalities. These are two important elements to success. Like most Specialists, you are not the greatest rainmaker, but once you have a client or prospect, you do a great job of keeping them.

The Diplomat's Business Strengths

You can also excel in retail, a service industry, or other people-oriented environments. Both outgoing and empathetic, you tend to be well liked, but you sometimes have a hard time asserting yourself and holding others accountable. Therefore, to successfully lead a company, you typically need to hire stronger, more results-oriented personalities to be sure deadlines are met, commitments are kept, and staff members follow through on duties.

Okay, so where does all this personality analysis leave you? It's not just a feel-good exercise. The best entrepreneurs know that the greatest knowledge is self-knowledge. With a better understanding of your strengths and weaknesses you can focus on a business where you can thrive instead of doing something that goes against your natural abilities. Remember, your business should meet your needs and your customers' needs. So the more you know about what makes you happy, the more successful you'll be at creating a fulfilling business experience. With a better understanding of your own personality, you can better leverage your strengths and work to improve your weak areas and limitations. If there are any skill gaps or personality gaps, you can fill these with your support team or staff or look to other business areas that are better suited to your strengths.

Know Your Success State

Another clue to deciphering the right business fit comes from thinking about what success looks like to you. Everyone's definition is different. Do you want to be in the limelight or will you feel fulfilled staying behind the scenes? Imagine what your ideal day as an entrepreneur would entail. Do you see yourself on countless lunch and dinner meetings? If so, sales or consulting may be right for you. Do you like to work alone? If so, a home-based online business may be a better fit. Do you see yourself managing a team of workers? Or do you see yourself working from the beach? Maybe your idea of success involves giving back and community work. Everyone's vision is different; make sure your business reflects that.

Tasha Monroe loved working with kids. She wanted to build a business that forged alliances with corporations to go into inner-city schools with skills training. It was the perfect blend of corporate funding and community service. However, Tasha realized that she hated the time-consuming work of trying to get corporations on board, the pitching, the selling of the concept, and then dealing with all the internal processes of each company to actually get paid. Because of those important demands, Tasha ended up with very little time to actually work with kids. Her goal was to build a venture that was heavily community focused, but the weight of dealing with administrative tasks she didn't like slowly crushed her love for the business. After two years, she abandoned her business, thinking that the idea just didn't work. Instead, Tasha could have outsourced the sales and pitching and focused on doing what she loves. At the time, she felt she couldn't afford it, but in retrospect, the investment would have handily paid off. You'll learn about other business-building strategies in later chapters. The point is that Tasha's vision for the business was completely different from the actual reality of the day-to-day operations, and that became a bad business mix for her. That doesn't always mean you should abandon your business; perhaps you can simply readjust your business model. Remember, any good business plan is fluid and constantly changing. Getting to the right fit can be an ongoing process.

Believe in Yourself

Another area that has to be airtight is your belief in yourself. An unwavering belief that you can do it and that you will succeed regardless of the rough patches in the journey is one of the best tools to carry along the way. If you have the sort of business that fits neatly into traditional business models, like a store or accounting firm, there are plenty of guides and training to help you. However, when you're blazing new trails, you may have to write your own book! Be your own training guide. To really do this, you have to deprogram yourself to break free from ideas, behaviors, patterns, and even people that will no longer serve you. When you are following a passion, and not a traditional model, you are a special kind of entrepreneur that is usually less understood and more often ridiculed. Listen to your intuition and let it sound louder than the no's and naysayers.

Don't be surprised if others are slow to come around. But trust that voice within to guide you.

To properly prepare yourself for the road ahead, you may have to get out your broom—not the witch one, but the symbolic one you use to sweep out the dust, dirt, and cobwebs of your life. If you're serious about turning your ideas into a real business, you have to create a clearing for success, a clearing in your life for prosperity, a clearing in your home to remove clutter, a clearing in your mind for positive thinking. Get rid of negative thinking and negative people.

When you do all that, then it's time to show and prove. Don't fret; there's plenty of advice in the rest of the book to teach you how. Performance and excellence must follow. Only by becoming the best in your field can you have long-term success with your company. Finding out your core competency and innate skills is the first step. Then you have to test and market-research your idea to make sure it's viable as a moneymaking business. To do so, you're going to need some important market-research know-how.

Mocha Mix
How I Found My Perfect Business Match

* * * * * * * * * * * * * * * * * * *

When I was growing up, everyone knew that if you needed someone to get the word out, you just had to tell me about it. I was a natural people person and I could think creatively. After a lot of corporate jobs, I knew there was something better for me out there, and I was very busy doing "publicity" for my church and my other friends who hosted events. I just didn't realize it. One day, my pastor commended me on the good turnout for an event and suggested I consider doing publicity as a regular business. It was my a-ha moment . . . straight from the Lord!

— CHERYL TOWNES, president of OnPointe Media, a
   public relations firm in Richmond, Virginia

I found my perfect business match with a lot of self-examination and looking at what it is that I enjoy doing. I know I enjoy helping people. My business provides drug testing services for companies, schools, and families. The idea came to me because it is a social issue that greatly concerns me.

— SHAQUANDA SPIVEY, president of SOLUTIONS Drug
   Testing Services, LLC, New Jersey (www.solutionsdts
   .com)

To help me make the right choice, I talked to others who already were where I aspired to be. I would advise others to ask plenty of questions and decide if that is truly the direction you want to go and if you are willing to take the steps to get there.

— Mia Sears, CEO of Posh VIP Ltd., Cincinnati, Ohio (www.posh-vip.com)

During a moment of epiphany, my own personal experiences collided with live observation and ideal timing. I immediately did thorough research tied to my idea, found a void for our product (a nutrient-enhanced flavored water beverage created with the hydration and dietary needs of expectant and new moms in mind), and set forward to determine exactly what I'd need to do to create the beverage, brand it, and sell it.

— Gretchen Cook-Anderson, CEO of Saphia Lifestyle Beverages, LLC, Maryland (www.saphiawater.com)

Both of my parents were musicians, so my siblings and I grew up with music in our lives. I became a music teacher in the school system, but I thought the ear-based learning system for young children didn't focus enough on reading music or understanding music theory. I decided to start my own program.

— Phoebe Simpson, co-owner of Piano Play, a music education program based in Los Angeles (www .pianoplaymusic.com)

Find a way to merge something you love to do with something you have training to do. If you can't, find a way to become as educated as possible about something you think you'll enjoy doing but have no experience in.
— Jasmine White, president, Urban P.O.W.E.R. Productions, a video production company in Maryland

Be honest about what you are searching for! Do you want a career/job or do you want to follow your passion? Make sure there is a need for your passion and you can provide a service.
— Yaa O. Whitmore, CEO of Your Own Way Consulting, a firm that coaches groups and individuals to proficiently try out for professional sports entertainment teams (www.yowconsulting.com)

My advice would be to first have a little knowledge about the business that you would like to get into. The love and passion for it will not be enough. You will have to know your industry from top to bottom. Do your research. The Internet is *free* and has a vast amount of resources for just about any service or trade. Be willing to pay the price for success and/or failure. Sometimes the two go hand in hand. Always consider the reality . . . that you may not be successful at what you choose, but it most certainly will lead to another opportunity presenting itself. Just make sure you are ready when it happens.
— Toni Scott Grant, CEO of Scott Phree, Inc., an online retail boutique based in Texas (www.scottphree .com)

A TREE GROWS IN BROOKLYN

Lisa Price, founder, president, and CEO of Carol's Daughter, a skin and hair care beauty line available in department stores like Macy's as well as Sephora and online at www.carols daughter.com.

Many, many moons ago when I was young, childless, carefree, and living single in Brooklyn, New York, my girlfriend Joyce Davis and I would engage in a monthly ritual. It involved walking to Lisa Price's house to get our Carol's Daughter supplies. I remember it as a ritual because it had to be carefully timed. You see, I was from the tree-lined streets of Queens and Joyce was from the quiet suburbs of Atlanta, and although we talked trash and walked like bad girls, we were punks at heart. And this part of Brooklyn was definitely not for punks. So we were not going to be there after dark. We wanted our mango soufflé without becoming mangled soufflé in the process. So every so often we would make our broad-daylight trek to the brownstone that housed Carol's Daughter during the designated shop hours. Lisa was well known in Brooklyn in the street- and craft-fair circles, but we liked the direct approach. We'd knock on the downstairs door and be greeted by Lisa and, right behind her, the smells of a lifetime. I'll never forget the day we watched Lisa scoop a fresh batch of body butter straight from her tub and into our clear glass jars.

So you can understand the sheer sense of pride I feel when I now walk into my local mall and into one of Carol's Daughter's six nationwide locations to purchase products for myself and my two children. A legacy is being made.

When I sat down with Lisa Price to interview her for this book at the same house where I once dropped in on those Saturday afternoons, she was still as fragrant as ever. She has the redolence of success, and I was captivated.

Lisa's now multimillion-dollar business was born out of her passion. Quite simply, she had a thing for moisturizers. "The way some women feel about hair products, that's the way I was about moisturizers. I always had a different moisturizer for the different seasons. I would wake up from my sleep to make butters," she says.

Today aspiring entrepreneurs dream of Lisa's accomplishments. She is the epitome of taking a side hustle born from a personal passion and growing it into a million-dollar business.

Lisa shares her advice for sweet success:

Be willing to make sacrifices for your business

There's a point as a business owner when you have to ask, "What more can I do to grow this business by myself?" It may be time to sacrifice your ego for the sake of helping your baby really grow. You will have to give up something for your business to have greater reach and greater impact.

Make sure your business fits your life vision

Ask yourself who you are in this scenario. Do you want to own the retail stores or do you want to be the shopkeeper? Do you want to deal with customers or be creative in the background? Know for sure who you want to be and maintain your identity so decisions are not made around you.

Consider partnerships to grow

A trusted friend suggested that I have lunch with Steve Stoute [the infamous former manager of rapper Nas turned business exec who founded Translation, a company that pairs pop stars with corporations that want to promote their brands. His clients include Jay-Z, and he brokered Beyoncé's endorsement deal with Tommy Hilfiger]. I had absolutely no idea why he wanted to meet with me, but I knew that if this friend suggested I take the meeting, I should. I knew about Steve's work with Reebok, the S. Carter line, and G-Unit, and the best that I could come up with was that he wanted me to create a fragrance for one of his clients. [Turns out he wanted to partner in her business, help secure investments celebrity endorsements from Will and Jada Smith, Mary J. Blige, and more]. I liked that he understood what it was like to be an entrepreneur. We were also on the same page about the future of the company.

If you are established and you have a following and you go into partnership or take on investors, everything that happens thereafter should be an evolution, not a re-creation.

Going big comes at a price

Now there's a process for launching new products that's so complicated that sometimes it's frustrating for me, for the artist part of me. I can't just whip up a batch of something and try it out on new customers anymore. When you go into mass production, products have to be stabilized and tested to make sure the ingredients don't separate over time. They have to be tested at different temperatures. They have to be in stability for three months.

Clearly identify your competitive advantage

For a long time, beauty companies were not concerned about African-American women as consumers. Now we're having a big impact in redefining beauty for African-American women and that has caused an upset in the market. For us to be in Sephora and Macy's is causing upset to the larger companies that ignored us for years. What they don't have is the value of the story—the story of Carol's Daughter. They don't have the personal connection that our customers have to me and the products. That personal connection, and our unique story, will keep us from being squashed.

Build your company so it can run without you

I can't do it all. I had to learn to delegate. Several years ago I was very ill. Everything shut down for two weeks and it scared me. I thought, this is dangerous. So I wrote everything down, from recipes to procedures, and I learned to delegate. It took a lot of pressure off me. Before I was creating, merchandising, ordering raw materials and supplies—everything! In that environment, it's hard to be creative.

Expect challenges with success

At times I'm fighting to find my voice in my own company. And I miss the creative side. I have to find something to satisfy my creative side, so I think I may make another baby! Maybe I'll start a private-label brand.

CHAPTER THREE

Will It Work? How to Properly Research and Test Your Business Idea

The best vision is insight.
—*Malcolm Forbes*

You think you have a brilliant service or product. But how do you know if there's a market or demand for it? Is it a great idea but not broad enough for a business? Is there side-hustle potential but not much else? All of these questions can be answered in your research phase.

Research is a blessing and a curse. The blessing part is that market research is the lynchpin for any viable business. It becomes the basis of the initial and full-blown business plans you will soon put together. It will guide your marketing materials, pricing, and networking efforts. But research is an area where many women get stuck. Analysis paralysis, I call it. Some time ago I met a young woman I'll call Kathy who was stuck. She had a gazillion business ideas—some of them ingenious! She hatched the idea of an Internet dating service for people with disabilities. She even had a great name for the company. Her youngest son had a disability and she was passionate about this idea. Plus, after years of trying to create a social life for her disabled son, she was well connected in that community. She knew people, had the inside perspective, and knew where to find her first customers! It was perfect—a brilliant idea. But Kathy was stuck in analysis paralysis. She never felt that she knew enough, researched enough, or explored enough to actually do something.

To make matters worse, while her body was paralyzed from moving forward, her mouth was wide open—she was telling everyone and their mama about her idea. Ladies, there's a critical difference between speaking about an idea with people who can help you move forward and talking to people whom you don't know well, who can't contribute to your process, and who aren't trustworthy about your brilliant business idea. I'm sure you know by now where this is going. For months and months I tried to coach her through the real roadblock—which had nothing to with research, by the way—and get her to do something. Do anything! My girlfriends and I were so tired of hearing about her do-nothingness over such a great idea that we jokingly said we were going to buy the website name and register the company name behind her back and do it ourselves! Hey, too slow, ya blow!

By the time she actually decided to do something, the domain name was long gone and someone had set up her exact same business idea. She never found out if the site was stolen by one of the myriad people she spoke to or just an unfortunate coincidence. My girlfriends and I later lamented that if we were the ones who stabbed her in the back and took her idea, at least we would have gladly sold her back the domain name and site. For a fee, of course. (Just kidding. Well, sort of! Hey, we're business-women!)

But there are two key learning points from Kathy's experience. One, she was absolutely correct that solid research is crucial. No business can survive without extensive market research. That's what you'll learn how to do in this chapter. But doing research for the sake of research is a waste of time. The research moves you closer to action. The research helps you fine-tune your idea, test it out, see where the gaps are, and then you absolutely go out there and do it.

The other key learning point from dear Kathy is that very few of us are reinventing the wheel. In fact, the majority of great ideas are simply improvements, adjustments, or upgrades to an existing product or service. A new spin on something old. And great ideas happen to loads of people. Often the only thing that differentiates you is actually acting on that idea! The secret to transforming an idea from a concept marinating in your head to real profit is *action*. Thomas Edison famously said, "Genius is one percent inspiration and ninety-nine percent perspiration." A great idea is key to your success, but thoughts alone, even if inspired by the good Lord himself, will get you nowhere. It's time to sweat!

This chapter will teach you some key avenues for market research, whether you are looking to bring a product to market or launch a new service-based business. Some of the processes will be the same, others will be very different. Just remember, you have the mind-set and ability to make it happen!

> **Tough Times Tip:** When there's a down market, focus on selling necessity goods and services. In good times or bad, consumers need staples like computers, food, and health-related products and services. Even high-end goods and services can do well. The trick is to avoid the middle market.

Products

Thousands of moms have become millionaires by inventing simple products after thinking about what would make their life easier. In 1997 Julie Aigner-Clark, a former English teacher and full-time mom, founded a company called Baby Einstein simply because she wanted videos that would expose babies to the arts and humanities. She cobbled together supplies, borrowed equipment, and filmed two videos in her own basement. Well, the requests came rolling in. Five years, ten videos, and $20 million in sales later, she and her husband sold Baby Einstein to Disney. Then there's Tamara Monosoff, who created the TP Saver—a little doohickey to keep your precocious toddler from unraveling all the toilet paper off the roll. I know you're thinking, *I could have thought of that!* And you're right, but Tamara did something about it! Now it's your turn.

To start, get a dedicated bound notebook to keep track of your ideas, conversations, sketches, and action plans. Not only is this a great way for you to maintain clarity on your idea but it is also a powerful business tool that is recommended by the United States Patent and Trademark Office. That's because a dated notebook with a well-documented record of your conversations and meetings with others will act as a record to validate your work and progress if someone should steal your idea or there are other problems and discrepancies down the road. And if someone is working independently from you to develop a similar idea, patent rights are granted to the person "most actively developing the product." So be active!

If you read some books on product development you'll see that the phases of the process can vary. If you haven't read those books, quite frankly I'm glad you spent your money on this one instead, and I'm going to tell you what they say. In the traditional framework, new product development, also known as the sequential or "over-the-wall" approach, typically involves the following phases: idea generation and validation, preliminary design, final design, process design, pilot production, and ramp-up. There are some more modern versions of this process, but essentially these are the core phases.

STEP ONE: ASK QUESTIONS

If you're in the idea generation and validation phase then you need to have a strong and clear idea of what your product is, always keeping in mind this key question: What problem does it solve?

Start by writing down the answers to these ten questions:

1. What is your idea?
2. How does it work?
3. What problem does it solve?
4. What are the possible product names?
5. What are your product's features?
6. What will your product look like? Draw a sketch.
7. What is your product's benefit? How will it help someone in their daily life?
8. What makes your product unique to the market?
9. Who is your target customer?
10. Can your product be expanded to other uses for other customers? If so, how?

If your answers to these questions reveal that the idea is viable and marketable, it's time to move on to the next step, research.

STEP TWO: RESEARCH, RESEARCH, AND RESEARCH

Before you can bring a product to market you need to know what's already out there. You don't want to waste time, money, and energy on something someone else already did. Toni Scott, the Houston-based owner of Scott Phree, an online boutique, was devastated when she realized that after several years planning her business, someone else owned the trademark to her original business name. "I admit, my research was lackluster. By the time I had invested money, time, and effort, the other company had filed for a trademark a mere four months before me. I lost the money and the trademark. I had credit cards, a website built, business checks, a business certificate, you name it, all in the company name I thought I had," Toni says.

To make sure this doesn't happen to you, you need to do a market search and a preliminary patent search. A market search lets you know if your idea or something similar is already being sold in stores, catalogs, or online. The preliminary patent search lets you know if someone else already has an intellectual claim to the idea or invention even if it hasn't made it to market yet. The good news is you can do most of this work from your own home via the Internet.

Start with a simple Google search. Use specific and obvious keywords and phrases first. Then switch it up. For example, if you want to launch a line of steak knives, start with "knife" and then search "steak knives" or "cutlery." Take a few minutes to learn how you can improve your search with Google by using "and" or adding quotation marks. Think of different synonyms to find phrasing alternatives. Use a thesaurus or www.synonym.com for ideas. Remember, this is a trial-and-error process. Try as many possible words for your product as you can before you come to any conclusions. Try other search engines, like Ask and

Yahoo. After you've done an exhaustive online search, its time to hit the stores!

The online retail market is only one aspect of your research; bricks-and-mortar retailers may have other products in stock. Your in-store research should include big box stores like Target and Wal-Mart, grocery stores, and drugstores, along with smaller independent shops.

Your mission is to answer these questions:

1. Does my product already exist?
2. What products are similar but not exactly the same? List the similarities and differences.
3. How does my product differ? Be specific.
4. Which stores sell these similar products? Write down the names and contact information.
5. Which manufacturers produce them? Write down their names and contact details too.
6. What is the price of these similar items? How does the price differ at different retailers and online?

After considering all of the above, ask yourself, is there still room for your product? If so, why? Remember, if your proposed product is already on the market, that doesn't necessarily mean you've hit a wall. Think about ways you can improve upon or differentiate your product. Write down these thoughts and ideas in your notebook. It's time to go to the next research level.

Preliminary Patent Search

Your patent search begins at the website of the United States Patent and Trademark Office (USPTO), www.uspto.gov. On the home page, look for "Patent Search." You may need to download the free plug-ins and image viewer software. You will need this to view images of the patent drawings. Once you've got your software in place, look for "Advanced Search." That's where you type in your keywords. Check the site for tips on helpful search terms and the correct use of quotation marks.

STEP THREE: BRINGING YOUR IDEA TO LIFE

Once you're ready to move forward with your idea, it's time to consider a prototype. This is a physical version of your idea. It can be a working model or close to it. Having a prototype makes sure everyone knows what you're talking about and it puts you in the ranks of serious businesspeople. When you approach an attorney, licensing company, or manufacturer down the road with a prototype in hand, you'll be well ahead of the scores of people with just an idea.

The prototype also helps you realize if your idea actually works as you conceived it.

Marsha Burnett, a sassy Brit from East London turned New York City diva, spent years planning, researching, developing, and launching her second business, Ensant (www.ensantlotions .com), a skin care line for expectant women. Marsha is a twenty-seven-year-old mother of two and wife of Len Burnett, a former publisher of *Vibe* and founder of *Uptown* magazine. "When the idea of having a skin care line actually began to take root, I needed to make sure that it was achievable. I don't have a qualification in skin care—except that I have skin and I buy cosmetics! I started by researching the cosmetics industry's rules and regulations and then I kept reading all of the labels on my favorite products," Marsha says.

Research is key. Marsha used the online white pages to look up manufacturers and suppliers. "I called fifty of them and asked for samples, brochures, and sometimes a tour of the facility. Then I started the same research process to find a formulator and packaging supplier. I had an idea of what I thought was missing from the market and I kept ordering brochures and bottle samples until I found what I liked. Then I asked everybody I knew for their opinions. It took me about nine months and a couple of mistakes to finalize my production team. All relationships take time to build and sometimes they won't be a good match. It's not always a bad thing to find this out. Use the experience and move on," she says.

Marsha wanted to create a skin care line for expectant women that not only remedied skin problems like stretch marks, acne, and melasma but also addressed two key concerns during pregnancy: stretching and tearing down below during delivery. Marsha's passion came from her own fear during her pregnancy that she would tear during delivery. It's every woman's worst nightmare. She became a student of perineal massage, which can help make your vaginal muscles more supple for stretching during birth, and felt there was a need for a better balm. At first she was making her own, mixing store-bought brands with other ingredients to make the balm longer-lasting or less greasy. Then she was inspired to create her own formula. After she launched Ensant, Marsha's real work began!

Tip: If you're in need of chemists, manufacturers, or prototype developers, go to www.thomasnet.com, a one-stop resource for everything you could possibly need. It has a database of 650,000 manufacturers, service providers, distributors, and others all broken down by state. And whether your prototype is made of plastic, wood, or metal, you can type your keywords and quickly find companies in the United States and Canada with just a few clicks.

COUNTING THE COSTS

Before you dive into product development, it's good to know some of the possible costs in the early days.

Preliminary patent or trademark search: We've walked you through some of the process for doing it yourself in this chapter. If you want to hire a professional it will cost you anywhere from $250 to $800.

Prototype development: Depending on the materials and complexity of your design, a professional prototype service can run you from a few hundred to thousands of dollars.

Market testing: This is where your friends and family can come in handy. You can easily put together your own informal focus groups. A professional focus group will cost you between $3,000 and $5,000 to pull off.

Patent: You can get a provisional patent with a $100 filing fee at the U.S. Patent and Trademark Office. If you are patient and detail oriented, you can draft and file for a patent yourself. Or you can expect to spend approximately $2,500 or more for a patent agent and $10,000 and up for a patent attorney.

Beware, ladies! There are scams out there. The Internet is brimming with companies that promise to take your idea to market for a fee. Some of these invention promotion companies charge from $1,000 to $30,000 or more. Even if they guarantee you a patent or your money back, be sure to ask for references before you sign a contract. The Federal Trade Commission offers some cautionary facts for consumers on invention promotion firms. Visit www.ftc.gov or call 877-FTC-HELP. Also consider these reminders:

1. **Anything that sounds too good to be true usually is.** Be leery of people who are way too enthusiastic or go overboard with promises.
2. **Get it in writing.** Make sure you have a written proposal. Read the fine print and check out the company's references.
3. **Get references and double-check them.** Always ask to speak to at least two other clients and make sure you call them. Since some questionable companies can use fake references, make sure you ask these references specific questions, like: What is your patent number? When was it issued? Where is your product sold? And then make sure you verify the answers.
4. **Use the government.** The Federal Trade Commission website has a pretty comprehensive rundown of bogus promises and specific responses to these claims. The USPTO (www.uspto .gov) also has a list of companies with complaints against them.

If you're launching a product, skip to "Market Research for Products and Services" on the following page. I'm going to address the service-industry launchers for a few minutes.

Services

Offering a service is one of the more common business routes. People love to pay others for things they don't want to do or don't know how to do. From accounting, financial planning, writing, and administration to concierge services, the service industry is a huge part of our economy. It also presents a great business opportunity if done correctly. Before launching a service-based business, you should ask yourself these questions:

1. Does my service already exist?
2. What services are similar but not exactly the same? List the similarities and differences.
3. How does my service differ? Be specific.
4. Who are my potential direct and indirect competitors? Is this service offered online? Write down the names and contact information.
5. What is the price of similar services? Does the price differ online and offline?

After considering all of the above, ask yourself if there's still room for your company. If so, why? If there's a demand, then there always will be enough customers to support several providers. Think about ways you can improve upon or differentiate your service by going upscale, budget friendly, or eco-conscious.

Market Research for Products and Services

Whether you are starting a product- or service-based business, getting the market research done correctly is important. Now, we're going to consider both product and service businesses together because you can follow much of the same advice to make it happen with either type of venture.

First let's review some of the preliminary research you should have already completed. By now, you should have clear, succinct answers to the following questions:

- **Why does my proposed business exist? What does it aim to accomplish?**
- **What are the specific short- and long-term goals?**
- **How will the business grow? How will you build it?**
- **What is the work to be done?**

If you answer those key questions you will have the basis for a vision, a mission statement, a list of objectives, strategies, and an action plan. You also need to figure out your pricing structure. People may want a service, but at what price? How much are people willing to pay for your product?

To help you figure out pricing, your target market, and so much more, you have to do some serious market research. Whether you've got a product or service, you need big-picture information to make sure your idea is feasible enough to take you to the next level. Are you sitting on a money-earning business idea or just side-hustle material?

THE NEXT LEVEL OF MARKET RESEARCH

Here's some Marketing 101. There are generally two sources of market research information: secondary data and primary data. Secondary data is information that has already been gathered and is now available to the public. That could include demographic data from the U.S. Census Bureau, newspaper articles, trade journals, or reports purchased from a marketing firm. Primary data is information that is specific to your product or service. It can come from focus groups, random interviews, telephone surveys, or e-mail blasts, and it tells you exactly what consumers like and dislike about your product.

Secondary Research

Here are a few great sources for secondary research.

1. **Census data (www.census.gov).** You can get some great population data here that can help you figure out how many people are in your target market. If you click on "Subjects A–Z" you can see all the reports available, information on everything from African-Americans to the elderly population. You can also search by your own keywords by using the "American Fact Finder" function. Census data is also available at your local library.

2. **The Internet, of course.** Use search engines with reckless abandon.

3. **Trade associations.** A trade association serving your industry can help you stay on top of industry trends. For example, if you're starting a concierge service, you could join the International Concierge and Errand Association (ICEA) or the National Association of Professional Organizers. You will receive insider news and stats.

4. **Professional market research outfits.** Type "market research" in your favorite search engine. Reports can cost anywhere from $500 to $5,000 depending on the industry and the depth of the report.

Primary Research

Once you've got your broader market research, its time to narrow your focus by going straight to your consumer.

Informal Focus Groups: These can be as informal as a get-together with friends and acquaintances or a more formal setup. Ask each attendee to bring a friend, and you might want to sweeten the deal with some snacks. That always entices me! You could also hold a raffle drawing or reward all participants with a gift certificate. Ask a friend if you can use the conference room at her office, or get a meeting room at the local library.

Norrinda Brown and her mom started using baking as their weekend escape from some serious life transitions and then turned it into a business plan for the Brown Betty Dessert Boutique in Philadelphia. Before they watched the dough rise on their business idea, they tested the market. "We wanted to see if our cakes would sell, so for months, we held tasting parties for friends and family," Norrinda explained in one interview. "We asked guests to write comments anonymously on cards." Those comments included sheer praise for the chefs, but also a few "too moist" or "too sweet" comments. Norrinda says her mother worked on the recipes until her focus groups revealed they had just the right amount of moistness, sweetness, and flavor. In 2007, Brown Betty was voted among the best of Philadelphia by a city magazine and a local newspaper.

To create your own winning focus groups, have a clear idea of what you want to accomplish. List the questions you want to ask. Consider: Have you seen anything like this before? What did you think of the service? Would you purchase this product or service? If not, why not? If there's a similar product or service out there, ask what would make someone buy yours instead. If yes, how much would you pay for it?

The group should have a moderator and someone else to take

notes. It's also a good idea to tape the session. Participants may be more comfortable giving honest feedback if you're not in the room. Others are brutally honest no matter who is around.

Charrisse Jones of Macon, Georgia, had a lot of success using her local church members to serve as her focus groups before she launched her concierge service. Charrisse knew what types of services she needed as a busy working mom, but she wanted to get a better idea of what other types of time-saving activities people were willing to pay for. More important, she needed to know how much customers would be willing to spend. She also asked questions about other service providers to get an idea of what people thought of her future competition. To help with her focus group, Charrisse contacted the local community college, which recommended a marketing student who was eager for the experience of facilitating a market research session. Charrisse made a few snacks and chose to leave the premises. "The results were eye-opening. Many of the things that I thought would be popular services weren't as in-demand as I thought. The focus groups helped me offer what people actually want, not what was in my own head," says Charrisse, whose company is now five years old and still thriving.

Have your participants sign a release form. You may be able to use their comments in future marketing materials.

You may also want to take your research to the streets. When I was the Wall Street reporter for the *New York Post,* the newspaper was famous for "Vox Pop," the term for the paper's "Voice of the People" report. I and other lucky reporters would head out to the streets of Manhattan to ask any man or woman we could find their opinion on our hot topic du jour. There's something unique and unfiltered about getting the everyday person's perspective. It is part of your job to do your own "Vox Pop," as it were, and then some.

1. Choose a public place where you can find your target market. If you're looking for teens, try the mall. If you're looking for professionals, an office building parking lot may be ideal.

2. Be sure to identify yourself and have plenty of business cards handy. There are a lot of kooks out there. And people don't always feel comfortable being randomly approached in the street.

3. Have your one-sentence description and pitch well rehearsed and ready to go. People on the street were going somewhere before you stopped them. Keep it brief. Have preprepared forms with all your questions on them.

4. After the interview make a few notations on the type of person you interviewed (mother with young child, older gentleman, etc.).

If walking up to strangers is not your style, you can get the "Vox Pop" effect by other methods. You can find message boards and bulletin boards for your desired group easily on the Internet. Create a new topic in a bulletin board and let people know what you're doing and that you would appreciate their thoughts and feedback. You can also use e-mail blasts the same way. Ask your contacts to forward your e-mail to anyone they think fits your target description. Put your questions in the e-mail body to make it easier for any respondents.

Direct mail surveys and telephone surveys are also options. You can purchase mailing lists or find market research firms that can script, field, and process a phone survey. Google "list brokers" to find mailing lists and "telephone surveys" or "call centers" to find phone lists. Depending on how elaborate they are, mail surveys can cost from $1 to $5 per mail piece, including development, graphic design, handling, and postage. Of course, you can save money by using your own mailing list and doing it yourself. Same for the telephone. This is particularly good if you're launching a service in a particular area. You can easily open the white pages and ask people about what they would like to see in the area.

These research ideas can help you get more than enough information to improve your decision-making skills, which make all the difference between success and failure. It's also a great starting point before spending your precious dollars on professional research if necessary.

Marsha Burnett's journey with Ensant, the maternity skin care line, involved tapping into local mom groups, e-mailing friends for feedback, and buying research reports on the maternity market. She tested every aspect of her product, from concept to packaging. Even though she started with her perineal massage balm, her market research opened her eyes to a whole line of products. But she consistently asked questions. "You are probably not reinventing the wheel, so somewhere out there is someone who has done either this or something similar before you. Ask other people about their experiences and listen to their opinions. Ultimately you will make the final decisions, but it doesn't hurt to listen; you might learn something," Marsha says.

Now that you know your idea is a feasible foundation for a business and you've got a prototype under way, it's time to put your ideas down on paper to create a two-page "starter" business plan and then brush up on some other important business skills.

THE STARTER BUSINESS PLAN

You know the old adage "If you fail to plan, you plan to fail"? Well, it's particularly true in business. Planning a business is not just a theoretical exercise, it's a pen-to-paper, must-do task as well. Many entrepreneurs mistakenly assume that a business plan is needed only if you are seeking funding from outside sources. The truth is, the business plan is for you. It's your guide to your vision and how you will execute it. It is the road map to chart your future course.

Just remember that this is only a starting point; you will create a more comprehensive business plan down the road. For now, your plan can be as few as eight to ten pages. This is more than enough space for a new business to concisely capture its vision and plan. If your plan includes a lot of rambling, go back and keep it simple.

Here are the key components to a basic business plan:

Executive Summary—This section is the single most important part of your plan. In a nutshell, it summarizes your particular market opportunity and the solution to a problem that your business offers. One way to look at the summary is to think of it as the story of your business. What need does your business fulfill? How can you best summarize your business in sixty seconds or less? What is your vision? (One or two pages.)

About the Business—This section includes the company's legal status, history, and trimmed-to-the-bone bios of the management team. (About one page.)

(Continued)

The Product (or Service)—This section covers the description and value proposition of the company's product or services. (About two pages.)

Market and Competition—This is where you show your depth of market knowledge by describing your market, analyzing its size and trends, and briefly describing your competitors. Be sure to clearly show the "pain" or the opportunity in the market and how your business will address it. Where is that part of the market broken or inefficient? How does it create an opportunity for you? What problem will your business solve? (About two pages.)

Technology (or Processes)—A condensed overview of the technology that underlies the product (or service). This should include the product's design, status, and road map in detail as well. For a service-based business, this may include details about how the service will be executed. (About one page.)

Sales and Marketing—How are people going to find out about the product/service, how will you engage with them to get them to pay for it, and how much does it cost? What unique marketing advantages will you have? What joint ventures or other alliances can you form? This is where you talk about how you will market your business and increase sales. (About two pages.)

Financials—A condensed description of the company's finances, showing real or projected sources of income and expenses. Later, the company will need more in-depth financials. (About one page.)

Mocha Mix
Researching, Testing, and Getting Started!

* * * * * * * * * * * * * * * * * *

The first thing I did was hit the trade shows. I found textile companies who would give me fabric without huge minimums. I also found manufacturers who would work with my production size.
— ERIN BRAXTON, president of Erin Braxton sleepwear and loungewear (www.erinbraxton.com)

Share your vision with those closest to you before you begin your venture. They will be the ones there to hold you up and support you when it gets tough.
— SHARON SAULS, CEO of SKY Neurological Rehabilitation, Maryland (www.skyneurorehab.com)

Do research on the area you want to start up in. Make sure you subscribe to the magazines or read the industry publications to make sure it is something you can breathe and sleep for years on end without getting bored.
— ROBIN OWENS, CEO of Executive Levels International, an executive search firm in Maryland (www.executivelevels.com)

Prepare yourself for the journey and let self-determination and blind faith be your guide. Your research should include finding a mentor, if possible, who is working toward or has achieved the *exact* same goal that you have in mind. People are always willing to share their success stories and help you. But they have to know that you need the help. If pride and bashfulness are your strong personality traits, entrepreneurship may not be for you.

— TONI SCOTT GRANT, CEO of Scott Phree, Inc., Texas (www.scottphree.com)

To start our business we took out a home equity loan to buy equipment and rent a space. We did our research and picked the Northern Liberties area of Philadelphia because it was affordable and was the neighborhood that was projected to grow the most in the next ten years.

— NORRINDA BROWN, co-owner of Brown Betty Dessert Boutique, Philadelphia (www.brownbettydesserts.com)

Examine your interests and strengths. Identify the business model first, write a business plan to validate the model, then incorporate and create a brand.

— MELINDA EMERSON, CEO of Quintessence Multimedia, Philadelphia (www.quintessenceinc.com)

My most critical steps for starting my business were writing down my vision, researching similar companies, and developing a marketing and business plan.

— LUCINDA CROSS, president of LC Associates, a virtual assistant firm (www.ultimatevasupport.com)

THE CROSSWORD QUEEN

Jan Buckner Walker is the president of Kids Across Parents
Down (KAPD), which produces a series of crossword puzzles
for kids and parents to do together (www.kapd.com)

*Jan Buckner Walker has always worked her workplace. The attorney-turned–
crossword creator thanks the frighteningly boring aspects of her old job for giving
her time to find her passion. Then when she wanted a cushion to pursue her
dream, she actually developed a proposed corporate restructuring at her own
firm to help cut costs. The proposal didn't include her job, and she thereby gave
herself a buyout.*

*As a former general counsel for a large corporation, Jan, who lives in sub-
urban Chicago, spent hours in large depositions for product liability cases. "If
you have sleeping problems, you should go to one of these. It's basically rows of
attorneys doing the* New York Times *crossword puzzle on the down low.
That's where the idea came to me for Kids Across Parents Down—a crossword
puzzle that families could do together. I just wrote it down on my idea list in my
PalmPilot and got on with things. Years later, after getting married, I was at an
awards dinner for Unsung Heroes and there was a black guy who edited crossword puzzles. My husband leaned over and said, 'Didn't you have an idea for a
crossword puzzle?' I called him to learn about how to get into the business. That
contact wasn't really fruitful. So I pitched a puzzle to my local newspaper, the*
Washington Post. *They bought the puzzle. I was in!"*

Jan shares her tips for side–hustle success:

Become an expert in your field

I knew nothing about making crossword puzzles. So I got on the Internet and went to bookstores. I started to study in the underground communities of cruciverbalists—people who talk all day about crossword puzzle making. I learned about conventions and grids. I started with an American grid, but after some field testing I found that people enjoy a more lighthearted challenge when working with their children. So I changed the format to something more like a Scrabble board. Parents loved it and kids loved it. I break all the traditional rules so it can be fun. I decided my brand would be different.

Look into syndication

With the *Washington Post* already on board, I was able to get syndicated in other papers, like the *Los Angeles Times* and major papers in Chicago and Atlanta.

Go after corporate business

I started to target corporations and restaurants to place the puzzle on their menus and placemats. I started with Cracker Barrel. I Googled the name of the vice president of marketing and then I called him constantly, mostly after hours, hoping the secretary would be gone for the day and he would answer his own phone. It is shameful the number of times I called and didn't get through; I never left messages, but one day he answered. Once again, I was in!

Learn about licensing

I used my legal background to create licensing agreements with Cracker Barrel and McDonald's. I license the rights to use the KAPD name for a fee plus a fee for constructing the puzzle. Now this is the core of my business.

Deal with setbacks

I had a book deal with Putnam. I was so excited. But a new publisher came in and she didn't want to do activity books, so my deal fell through. I was devastated. I was in a serious funk for eight days. Then I slowly pulled out of my fetal ball. I thought, "You are the only employee of this company, and if you are sitting in a corner rocking back and forth your company will be shut down. Can you afford to be shut down for days? I don't think so. So you better get up." I had to dust myself off and get another contract.

Claim your new identity

I was always a lawyer. It was a tough process for me to identify myself as an entrepreneur. It was very hard for me to say, "I'm an entrepreneur." There is a lot of sleeplessness and perspiration. And the whole "eat what you kill" idea is scary. But you are putting something in the world that never existed before or you are optimizing something that is already in the world and launching it on your own. I don't think the urge to do that can be satisfied at a job.

Give to the world

KAPD is my gift to the universe. No idea has ever come to me the way this one did. It wasn't something I organically sat down and planned. It blossomed suddenly. It was a gift and I'm a guardian of it. I take that responsibility seriously. I'm attentive spiritually to what I'm supposed to be doing, and the more I'm attentive, the more blessings come to me.

Push past your personality

I make puzzles, and that's a very heads-down thing to do, so I'm not necessarily used to talking to people. I have to work at that.

Don't be afraid to release the brake

For years I had this emergency brake on my life because it was a safe and protected place to be. In order to move forward you have to take the brake off and just see. Everybody's brake is different—lack of self-confidence, your "inside the box" paradigm, your perception of your finances, your perception of how your family construct is limiting to you—my children, my husband, or my sick mom. If you cozy up to these reasons you will not go anywhere.

Watch the company you keep

In this world there are propellers and rudders. Propellers are elevating and energizing. They push you forward. Then there are rudders, the people who always mess it up for you—sometimes these are family members. If you have a rudder in your life, make sure there's a good reason. For example, I'm with this rudder because she is my mother and I have a personal credo that says I have to be a responsible daughter. But you know that she is a rudder. Don't invest the emotional energy in a conversation with a rudder.

CHAPTER FOUR

Other Paths to Entrepreneurship: Buying a Business and Franchises

Life is not about finding yourself.
Life is about creating yourself.
—*George Bernard Shaw*

There's more than one way to become a business owner. Some people aren't interested in the grueling start-up phase with the sleepless nights, often nonexistent revenues, and trial-and-error learning curve with no experience or little support. So before you get too far into the process, you may want to consider if buying or buying into an existing business or purchasing a franchise is a better route for you.

Of course, when you buy an existing business you give up a lot more creative control and flexibility than you would have starting your own business, and you are stepping into someone else's rules about how the business should be run. It also usually takes more up-front cash to go this route, but you have the benefit of an established name, an established reputation, and less risk. With that said, bankers are more likely to give you financing if you're buying a franchise or an existing business with a proven track record. Let's consider these other business ownership options:

Buying a Franchise

Many of the businesses you see every day, like 7-Eleven, Subway, and Dunkin' Donuts, are franchise-run operations. When you buy a franchise, you pay a hefty franchise fee for the right to open a store in a particular location and then you fork over a percentage of your monthly gross earnings in royalty fees to the holding company. Franchise fees can range from $25,000 and up, depending on the franchisor. McDonald's is famously known for its half-a-million-dollar franchise fee. Annual royalty fees can range from 3 percent to 10 percent. Typically, the larger the royalty fee you pay, the more support services you receive.

You pay more up-front, but you are buying name recognition and a service reputation. Instead of building a brand, you simply buy an established one. You get training, operational support, and marketing assistance. You also buy purchasing power. A good franchisee can take advantage of the buying power of the entire company to negotiate prices for everything she needs at significantly lower levels than she could achieve as an independent operator. This applies not only to initial furniture and equipment purchases, but also to the supplies, inventory, uniforms, and everything else she'll need on an ongoing basis.

Alicia Marks of Long Island, New York, always loved working with children and wanted to open a day care center. Through her work at the town superintendent's office, she had firsthand knowledge of a new development project in the area that was zoned to include a day care facility. When Tutor Time, a franchise-operated day care center, landed the contract for the space, the only thing missing was a franchisee to run the center. Alicia thought this was her chance.

Alicia and her husband applied to be a franchisee for Tutor Time. They had to complete a lengthy application and then face an all-important interview where they knew they had to sell themselves as the best pick. After they were approved, they paid a $40,000 franchise fee. Alicia borrowed $25,000 with an SBA loan and came up with the rest from savings and loans from family. Her franchise royalties are 6 percent per month.

Although Alicia knew the type of franchise she wanted to open, you may need to do some research. Just like with any other business opportunity, you need to find the right match for your skills and interests and your lifestyle. You should do some of the same self-examination of your strengths and weaknesses as discussed in previous chapters for start-up entrepreneurs. Be honest here—you don't want to pick the wrong franchise and later discover you're trapped in a legal obligation that's difficult to get out of.

It's also a good idea to make a list of all the things you enjoy doing and compare that list to the type of franchise you're considering. Is it a good fit? For example, if you like to vacation or beachcomb during the summer, will a franchise where you have to be there every weekend actually suit your lifestyle? By taking the time to create a firm picture of what you're looking for, you'll avoid getting involved with a franchise that looks good on the surface but really doesn't fit your life. Consider a free consultation with a service like Franchise Inc. Call 800-961-0420 or visit www.franchiseinc.com.

Marcia Robinson, a high-earning Wall Street executive, researched for about a year before buying an Amazon Café franchise. Amazon Café offers healthy alternatives to fast food with smoothies, wraps, and salads and was a fast-growing franchise in the Northeast. She began her research online, sifting through the thousands of franchise opportunities and looking for a good fit. Based on some trends in her local area she thought a restaurant with healthy food items would be a good choice. She wanted an opportunity that didn't necessarily require that she actually work in the location herself or have any particular expertise in the field. Then she looked at the capital and net worth requirements to whittle her list down even more. When Marcia came to a short list of possibilities, she hit the streets, actually visiting franchises like Quiznos and Subway during off-peak hours to speak directly with owners about their experiences. All the while she continued to familiarize herself with industry trends in the restaurant field and even subscribed to *Restaurant News,* a popular trade magazine. After her research and negotiations were complete, Marcia paid a $29,000 up-front franchise fee and had a sliding royalty fee that started with 3 percent and then moved up to 5 percent in three years.

Get a Plan of Attack

Once you know what you want out of a franchise, it's time to create a strategic plan of attack. This plan will include an entry strategy, a long-term strategy, and an exit strategy.

Your entry strategy gets you into a business with little difficulty and sets you up for success. This includes finding and buying the right franchise, getting it up and running without depleting all your financial resources, and learning the ins and outs of the business.

Your long-term strategy is your road map to success. Here you figure out your extended goals for the business and how you would like to fit the business into your life, both now and in the future. How do you see yourself living five or ten years down the road? Any business you buy should enable you to reach these goals and give you the life you want.

Your exit strategy is your "out." This is where you decide how you will get out of the business. Will you sell the franchise or pass it down to someone in your family? Although it might seem a little hasty, knowing how you want it all to end someday is a necessary part of selecting the right franchise for you.

Only after you have completed your self-evaluation and your strategic plan will you finally be ready to consider what you should expect from a franchisor.

WHAT YOU CAN EXPECT

While it's your job to work hard and make your business a success, your franchisor has a certain obligation to help along the way. Here are eleven things to consider when investigating different franchises.

1. **A proven system of success.** If the franchisor's system isn't strong and proven to work, don't pay for it. Don't let *your* franchise fees fund *their* learning process!

2. **A commitment to quality products and services.** Stay away from companies that are more interested in selling franchises than they are in supporting their system and providing quality goods. This is where your field research—speaking to existing operators—will come in handy.

3. **Information provided before you buy.** A franchisor should answer all of your questions and meet with you several times before you sign the agreement. Some details might not be available until you sign on the dotted line, but they shouldn't intentionally withhold information.

4. **A vision you believe in.** You should like your franchisor, and their vision should be compatible with your own. You need to feel comfortable with the direction they will take in the future.

Businesses change all the time, so pick a franchisor with a vision you can endorse.

5. **A recognizable name.** It's best to select a franchisor with a well-known trademark to maximize your potential for success. There may be greater growth potential with a newer franchisor, but a greater risk of failure goes with it.

6. **A fair agreement.** Most franchise agreements favor the franchisor, of course, but your rights must be protected at the same time. Find a franchise that recognizes your equity rights in the business that you will work hard to create. Make sure you have an attorney who is familiar with business contracts to review your agreements. Though most of the contract is standard, some items, such as the amount you contribute to the marketing budget and the right to buy in other areas, may be negotiable.

7. **Excellent training.** Find a franchisor with a commitment to long-term training. This is where a lot of franchisees feel they get the short end of the stick. Training should be low-cost or free, as part of your agreement. Your franchisor should also make frequent visits to your location to get a feel for your area, which will enable them to tailor their assistance to your unique needs.

8. **Strong resources.** Make sure your franchisor has the resources to help you if you ever get into financial trouble. Will they come up with ways to help you increase sales? Can they help you sell your franchise when the time comes? A strong head office is also important. Does your franchisor have the means to do their job properly? If a franchisor doesn't have the resources to gain market penetration or build a brand name, stay away.

9. **No litigation woes.** Although litigation isn't automatically a bad sign, be sure that any litigation doesn't affect your fran-

chisor's ability to help you do your job. Look for patterns in litigation. If the same type of lawsuit has been filed over and over by past franchise owners, take it as red flag. There's a real weakness in the system. At the time of Marcia's research, she learned from speaking to franchise owners that a class action suit had been recently filed by the franchise owners against a top-name franchisor that she was seriously considering. She struck them from her list.

10. **A rigorous selection process.** Each franchisee is a reflection of the overall system. Steer clear of a franchisor that will sell to anyone with the right amount of money. Your reputation is on the line if weak links in the system affect your business.

11. **Franchisee satisfaction.** Are most of the franchisees in the system happy with their choice? Are they successful and would they recommend the business to others? Investigate some very successful franchisees, some who are doing poorly, and some who are out of business to get a true overall picture of the opportunity.

Buying a franchise doesn't completely protect you from the ups and downs of the early days of business ownership. About a year after signing her franchise agreement, Alicia Marks opened the doors to her brand-new ten-thousand-square-foot day care center with an impressive eighty-three enrolled children and $50,000 in a discretionary fund. But the cost of supplies, maintenance, and payroll came fast and furious and quickly drained that fund in the first two months. And although she had eighty-three kids, the tuition payment for nearly 90 percent of her students was subsidized by the state. Alicia took a lot of pride in the fact that she was able to provide quality day care at affordable prices to her community by accepting state-subsidized tuition payments, but she didn't realize that state agencies are very slow to pay. At one point, her payments from the state were forty-five to sixty days past due and she couldn't meet her payroll. "It was a very difficult time. I had this money coming, but no one would give me a bridge loan in the meantime to meet payroll. I was putting my own money in, to the detriment of my personal finance and credit situation, just to pay bills. Checks were bouncing all over the place. We were in way over our heads. If it hadn't been for my family helping us, we'd have closed down within four months," says Alicia. "The two weeks of training we received certainly were not enough."

Ten years later, Alicia has a different story. Her Tutor Time day care center in Amityville, New York, is the pride of the local community. All her loans, including those from her family, have been paid off. And even though she still has a high subsidized rate, she went after contracts with local school districts that needed to outsource their pre-K programs due to lack of space. Alicia now operates pre-K programs for two school districts in her center. After being nearly crippled by slow payments from the state and learning that other day care centers were being put out of business for the same reason, Alicia joined forces with other day care owners to petition the county legislature for a new law that mandates prompt payment from the county and state to day care centers. The Prompt Payment Law went into effect in 2007.

Build-out costs can be another money burner with a franchise. After you find an approved location, it has to be "built out" to suit your business—refrigerators may be needed, display counters, new electrical wiring—and then there's the point-of-sale or accounting system and other equipment. When Marcia Robinson signed her franchise agreement, and the lease for lobby restaurant space in a busy downtown high-rise office building, the estimates she received for build-out costs were about $125,000. The final costs, nearly two years later when she actually opened, were closer to $175,000—money she paid out-of-pocket. She had a $35,000 savings cushion for the business, but it was quickly drained. "Things just come out of nowhere," she says. Marcia found herself using lunch breaks at the office to run downtown to the café and help with deliveries. Keeping good employees and retraining was another challenge. "A franchise can help you attract more customers, but don't assume you'll always escape all the sweat work and difficulties of opening a business," she says.

Buying an Existing Business

In most cases, buying an existing business is less risky than starting from scratch. When you buy a business, you take over an operation that's already generating cash flow and profits. You have an established customer base and reputation, and employees who are familiar with all aspects of the business. And you don't have to reinvent the wheel—setting up new procedures, systems, and policies—since a successful formula for running the business has already been put in place.

On the downside, buying a business is often more costly than starting from scratch. However, it's often easier to get financing to buy an existing business with some sort of earning record. In addition, buying a business may give you valuable legal rights, such as patents or copyrights, which can prove very profitable. Of course, there's no such thing as a sure thing—and buying an existing business is no exception. If you're not careful, you could get stuck with obsolete inventory, uncooperative employees, and a bum deal.

Tanesha Barnes, an esthetician in Bethel, Connecticut (www .tbarnesbeauty.com), took her big leap in entrepreneurship by buying a hair salon in her old Connecticut neighborhood, looking to bring savvy stylists from the city along with a day spa to the small town on the rise. Tanesha paid $6,000 for the salon, pooling funds with her ex-husband and borrowing some from her parents. "I put about ten thousand dollars in renovations into the space—new floors, equipment, and other cosmetic upgrades. I was on my hands and knees pushing up tiles," Tanesha says. She opened Solace Salon lifestyle and day spa in 2003. Depending on the type of business you buy, you have to really decide what you are buying. Are you purchasing the clients, the employees, the equipment, or the brand name? With a hair salon the clients are often attached to their stylists, so keeping key stylists was critical for Tanesha's early success. "The hair portion of the business was very complicated. I was too busy overseeing staff to market the business the way I wanted to and it was very hard to find reliable people," she says. Tanesha quickly learned that inheriting employees or finding solid new ones can be a challenge whether you buy or start a new business.

Tanesha's research prior to buying the business didn't uncover the equipment upgrades in hair dryers and electrical systems that the salon required. Within three to four years, however, things really took off with the salon, but Tanesha quickly learned that buying an existing business doesn't mean you avoid the start-up pains of entrepreneurship.

After getting frustrated at a never-on-time esthetician, Tanesha started doing facials herself and six months later obtained her license and became the in-salon esthetician. Tanesha sold the salon after five years. "I got a divorce. My lifestyle changed so I decided to focus on the esthetician side of my business. I built a skin care studio and day spa onto my home," she says. Later, she also opened a second skin care studio in Brooklyn, New York, and now markets her T. Barnes skin care line.

To make sure you get the best deal when buying an existing business, be sure to follow these steps:

MAKE THE RIGHT CHOICE

I just can't say this enough: buying the perfect business starts with choosing the right type of business for you. Fit still matters. Look at an industry you're familiar with and understand. Think long and hard about the types of businesses you're interested in and which best matches your skills and experience. Tanesha's work experience centered around event planning and marketing in New York City. She had a lot of experience pulling together all different sorts of people, from stylists to celebs, and products to make an event go well. She thought those skills would translate well to managing a salon. Also consider the size of business you are looking for in terms of employees, number of locations, and sales. Tanesha decided to start small and go back to a small town with little similar competition. Next, pinpoint the geographical area where you want to own a business. Think about what type of labor pool there is and the costs of doing business in that area, including wages and taxes, to make sure they fit with your budget and comfort level. Once you've chosen a region and an industry to focus on, investigate every business in the area that meets your requirements. Start by looking in the local newspaper's classified section under "Business Opportunities" or "Businesses for Sale." You can also run your own "Want to Buy" ad describing what you are looking for. Remember, just because a business isn't listed doesn't mean it isn't for sale. Talk to business owners in the industry; many of them might not have their businesses up for sale but would consider selling if you made them an offer. Put your networking abilities and business contacts to use, and you're likely to hear of other businesses that might be good prospects. There are also some great websites to help you. Start with an Internet search of "business for sale."

GET PROFESSIONAL HELP

Contacting a business broker is another way to find businesses for sale. Most brokers are hired by sellers to find buyers and help negotiate deals. If you hire a broker, he or she will charge you a commission—typically 5 to 10 percent of the purchase price. The assistance brokers can offer, especially for first-time buyers, is often worth the cost. However, if you are really trying to save money, consider hiring a broker only when you are near the final negotiating phase. Brokers can offer assistance in several ways.

1. **Prescreening businesses for you.** Good brokers turn down many of the businesses they are asked to sell, either because the seller won't provide full financial disclosure or because the business is overpriced. Going through a broker helps you avoid these risks.

2. **Helping you pinpoint your interest.** A good broker serves as a business-buying coach and starts by finding out about your skills and interests, then helps you select the right business for you. With the help of a broker, you may discover that an industry you had never considered is the ideal one for you.

3. **Negotiating.** The negotiating process is really when brokers earn their keep. They help both parties stay focused on the ultimate goal and smooth over any problems that may arise.

4. **Assisting with paperwork.** There's a lot of it. And brokers know the latest laws and regulations affecting everything from

licenses and permits to financing and escrow. They also know the most efficient ways to cut through red tape, which can slash months off the purchase process. Working with a broker reduces the risk that you'll neglect some crucial form, fee, or step in the process.

BUILD A TEAM

Whether you use a broker or go it alone, you will definitely want to put together an acquisition team—your banker, accountant, and attorney—to help you. These advisers are essential to what is called "due diligence," which means reviewing and verifying all the relevant information about the business you are considering. When due diligence is done, you will know just what you are buying and from whom. The preliminary analysis starts with some basic questions. Why is this business for sale? What is the general perception of the industry and the particular business, and what is the outlook for the future? Does—or can—the business control enough market share to stay profitable? Are raw materials needed in abundant supply? How have the company's product or service lines changed over time?

You also need to kick the tires, so to speak, by assessing the company's reputation and the strength of its business relationships. Talk to existing customers, suppliers, and vendors about their relationships with the business. Are they happy? About to sever ties? Contact the Better Business Bureau, industry associations, and licensing and credit-reporting agencies to make sure there are no complaints against the business.

If your preliminary research looks good, your team needs to dig in to the numbers by examining the business's potential returns and its asking price. Whatever method you use to determine the fair market price of the business, your assessment of the business's value should take into account such issues as the business's financial health, its earnings history, and its growth potential, as well as its intangible assets (for example, brand name and market position).

To get an idea of the company's anticipated returns and future financial needs, ask the business owner and/or accountants to show you projected financial statements. Balance sheets, income statements, cash flow statements, and tax returns for the past three years are all key indicators of a business's health. These documents will help you conduct a financial analysis that will spotlight any underlying problems and also provide a closer look at a wide range of less tangible information.

Sixteen Things to Consider Before Buying a Business

Use this brief checklist of items you should evaluate to verify the value of a business before buying it. This list doesn't cover everything, but it's a good start.

1. **Inventory.** This is all the products and materials inventoried for resale or use. Important note: You or a qualified representative should be present during any examination of inventory. You should know firsthand the status of inventory, what's on hand at present, and what was on hand at the end of the last fiscal year and the one preceding that. You should also have the inventory appraised. After all, this is a hard asset and you need to know what dollar value to assign it. Also, check the inventory for salability. How old is it? What is its quality? What condition is it in? Keep in mind that you don't have to accept the value of this inventory—it is subject to negotiation. If you feel it is not in line with what you would like to sell, or if

it is not compatible with your target market, then by all means bring those points up in negotiations.

2. **Furniture, fixtures, equipment, and building.** This includes all products, office equipment, and assets of the business. Get a list from the seller that includes the name and model number of each piece of equipment. Then determine its present condition, market value when purchased versus present market value, and whether the equipment was purchased or leased. Find out how much the seller has invested in improvements and maintenance in order to keep the facility in good condition. Figure out if any changes will be needed to the building or layout in order for it to suit your needs.

3. **Copies of all contracts and legal documents.** Contracts would include all lease and purchase agreements, distribution agreements, subcontractor agreements, sales contracts, union contracts, employment agreements, and any other instruments used to legally bind the business. Also, evaluate all other legal documents, such as articles of incorporation, registered trademarks, copyrights, patents, etc. If you're considering a business with valuable intellectual property, have an attorney evaluate it. In the case of a real estate lease, you need to find out if it is transferable, how long it runs, its terms, and if the landlord needs to give his or her permission for assignment of the lease.

4. **Articles of incorporation.** If the company is a corporation, check to see what state it's registered in and whether it's operating as a foreign corporation within its own state.

5. **Tax returns for the past five years.** Many small-business owners make use of the business for personal needs. They may buy products they personally use and charge them to the business or take vacations using company funds, go to trade shows with their spouses, etc. You have to use your analytical skills,

and those of your accountant, to determine what the actual financial net worth of the company is.

6. **Financial statements for the past five years.** Have your accountant evaluate these statements, including all books and financial records, and compare them to their tax returns. This is especially important for determining the earning power of the business. This is why you need an experienced accountant who's familiar with accounting rules in your industry. He needs to closely examine the sales and operating ratios and compare them against industry ratios, which can be found in annual reports produced by companies like the Risk Management Association and Dun and Bradstreet. Access these at your local library.

7. **Sales records.** Although sales will be logged in the financial statements, you should also evaluate the monthly sales records for the past thirty-six months or more. Break down sales by product categories if several products are involved, as well as by cash and credit sales. This is a valuable indicator of current business activity and provides some understanding of cycles that the business may go through. Compare the industry norms of seasonal patterns with what you see in the business. Also, obtain the sales figures of the ten largest accounts for the past twelve months. If the seller doesn't want to release his or her largest accounts by name, it's fine to assign them a code. You're only interested in the sales pattern.

8. **Complete list of liabilities.** Consult an independent attorney and accountant to examine the list of liabilities to determine potential costs and legal ramifications. Find out if the owner has used assets such as capital equipment or accounts receivable as collateral to secure short-term loans and if there are liens by creditors against assets, lawsuits, or other claims. Your

accountant should also check for unrecorded liabilities such as employee benefit claims, out-of-court settlements being paid off, and the like.

9. **All accounts receivable.** This refers to money due to the company. Break them down by thirty days, sixty days, and ninety days past due and beyond. Checking the age of receivables is important because the longer the period they are outstanding, the lower the value of the account.

10. **All accounts payable.** Like accounts receivable, accounts payable should be broken down by thirty days, sixty days, and ninety days past due. This is important in determining how well cash flows through the company. If there are payables more than ninety days old, you should check to see if any creditors have placed a lien on the company's assets.

11. **Debt disclosure.** This includes all outstanding notes, loans, and any other debt to which the business has agreed. See, too, if there are any business investments on the books that may have taken place outside of the normal area. Look at the level of loans to customers as well.

12. **Merchandise returns.** Does the business have a high rate of returns? Has it gone up in the past year? If so, can you isolate the reasons for returns and correct the problem(s)?

13. **Customer patterns.** If this is the type of business that can track customers, you will want to know specific characteristics concerning current customers, such as: How many are first-time buyers? How many customers were lost over the past year? When are the peak buying seasons for current customers? What type of merchandise is the most popular?

14. **Marketing strategies.** How does the owner obtain customers? Does he or she offer discounts, advertise aggressively, or conduct public-relations campaigns? You should get copies of all

sales literature to see the kind of image that is being projected by the business. When you look at the literature, pretend that you are a customer being solicited by the company. How does it make you feel? This can give you some idea of how the company is perceived by its market.

15. **Advertising costs.** Analyze advertising costs. It is often better for a business to postpone profit at year-end until the next year by spending a lot of money on advertising during the last month of the fiscal year.

16. **Location and market area.** Evaluate the location of the business and the market area surrounding it. This is especially important to retailers, who draw the majority of their business from the primary trading area. You should conduct a thorough analysis of the business's location and the trading areas surrounding the location, including economic outlook, demographics, and competition. For service businesses, get a map of the area covered by the business. Find out, based on the locations of various accounts, if there are any special requirements for delivering the product or any transportation difficulties encountered by the business in getting the product to market.

DETERMINING A FAIR PRICE

Once you've had a deeper look at the company's assets and liabilities, it's time to come to agreeing on a price. This can be an emotionally charged decision for an existing business owner. The owner has one idea of how much the business is worth, while you, the buyer, will typically have another viewpoint. Each party is dealing from a different perspective and usually the one who is best prepared will have the most leverage when the process enters the negotiating stage.

Keep in mind that most sellers determine the price for their business arbitrarily or through a special formula that may apply to that industry only. Either way, there usually aren't very many solid facts upon which to base their decisions.

Price is a very hard element to pin down. There are a few factors that will influence price, such as economic conditions. Usually, businesses sell for a higher price when the economy is expanding and for a much lower price during recessions. Motivation is also an important factor. How badly does the seller want out? If the seller has many personal financial problems, you may be able to buy the business at a discount rate by playing the waiting game. On the other hand, you should never let the seller know how badly you want to buy the business. This can negatively affect the price you pay.

Beyond these factors, you can determine the value of a business using several different methods, which are discussed below. There are some hard-core methods to assign value. These include:

MULTIPLIERS

Simply put, some owners gauge the value of their business by using a multiplier of either the monthly gross sales, monthly gross sales plus inventory, or after-tax profits. While the multiplier formula may seem complex and quite accurate to begin with, if you delve a little deeper and look at the components used to arrive at the value, there is actually very little to substantiate the arrived-at price.

Most of the multipliers aren't based on fact. For example, individuals within a specific industry may claim that certain businesses sell at three times their annual gross sales or two times their annual gross sales plus inventory. Depending on which formula the owner uses, the gross sales are multiplied by the appropriate number, and a price is generated.

Of course, you can check the monthly sales figure by looking at the income statement, but is the multiplier an accurate number? After all, it has been determined arbitrarily. There usually hasn't been a formal survey performed and verified by an outside source to arrive at these multipliers.

Don't place too much faith in multipliers. If you run across a seller using the multiplier method, use the price only as an estimate and nothing more.

BOOK VALUE

Book value is a fairly accurate way to determine the price of a business, but you have to exercise caution when using this method. To arrive at a price based on the book value, all you have to do is determine the company's net worth—that is, find out what the difference is between its assets and its liabilities. This usually has been done already on the balance sheet. The net worth is then multiplied by one or two to arrive at the book value.

This might seem simple enough. To check the number, all you have to do is list the company's assets and liabilities. Determine their value, arrive at the net worth, and then multiply that by the appropriate number.

Assets usually include any unsold inventory, leasehold improvements, fixtures, equipment, real estate, accounts receivable, and supplies. Liabilities can be anything. They might even include the business itself. Usually, they include unpaid debts, uncollected taxes, liens, judgments, lawsuits, bad investments—anything that will create a cash drain on the business.

Now here is where it gets tricky. In the balance sheet, fixed assets are usually listed by their depreciated value, not their replacement value. Therefore, there really isn't a true cost associated with the fixed assets, which can create very inconsistent values. If the assets have been depreciated over the years to a level of zero, there isn't anything on which to base a book value. This is where having professional accountants come in handy.

RETURN ON INVESTMENT

The most common means of judging any business is by its return on investment (ROI), or the amount of money the buyer will realize from the business in profit after debt service and taxes. However, don't confuse ROI with profit. They are not the same thing. ROI measures how well a company uses its capital to generate profit. It looks at how much profit or cost saving is realized for any given use of money. Profit is a yardstick by which the performance of the business is measured.

Typically, a small business should return anywhere from 15 to 30 percent on investment. This is the average net in after-tax dollars.

The wisdom of buying a business lies in its potential to earn money on the money you put into it. You determine the value of that business by evaluating how much money you are going to earn on your investment. The business should have the ability to pay for itself. If it can do this and give you a return on your cash investment of 15 percent or more, then you have a good business. This is what determines the price. If the seller is financing the purchase of the business, your operating statement should have a payment schedule that can be taken out of the income of the business to pay for it.

Does a 15 percent net for a business seem high? Everybody wants to know if a business makes two, three, or ten times profit. They hear price–earning ratios tossed around and forget that such ratios commonly refer to companies listed on the stock exchange.

Small businesses are different. The small business should typically earn a bigger return because the risk of the enterprise is higher. The important thing for you, as a buyer of a small business, is to realize that regardless of industry practices for big business, it's the ROI that you need to worry about most. Is it realistic? If the price is realistic for the amount of money you have to invest, then you can consider it a viable business.

THE ART OF THE DEAL

Deciding on a price, however, is just the first step in negotiating the sale. Even more important is how the deal is structured. Some acquisition experts suggest that you should be ready to pay 30 to 50 percent of the price in cash and finance the remaining amount.

You can finance through a traditional lender, or sellers may agree to "hold a note," which means they'll accept payments over a period of time, just as a lender would. Many sellers like this method because it assures them of future income. Other sellers may agree to different terms—for example, accepting benefits such as a company car for a period of time after the deal is completed. These methods can cut down the amount of up-front cash you need. Always have an attorney review any arrangements for legality and liability issues.

The final purchase contract should be structured with the help of your acquisition team. The contract must be all-inclusive and should allow you to rescind the deal if you find at any time that the owner intentionally misrepresented the company or failed to report essential information. It's also a good idea to include a noncompete clause in the contract to ensure that the seller doesn't open a competing operation down the street.

Remember, you have the option to walk away from a negotiation at any point in the process if you don't like the way things are going. If you don't like the deal, don't buy. Even if you've spent considerable time looking at something, it doesn't mean you're under any obligation to buy it.

> **Tough Times Tip:** Remember, an economic downturn can be a great buying opportunity. It's all about finding the right motivated seller. Experts overwhelmingly agree that strong synergies and solid company fundamentals are often more important than timing. A fundamentally sound company can withstand a recession and come out even stronger than before. A downturn is also a good time to get seller financing. In these markets a seller knows he needs to have something vested in the deal to prove the business's long-term success. You can also ask for an "earn-out." That's where the seller receives less up front and gets additional money based on the company's performance.

ALTERNATIVES TO CASH

Short on cash? Try these alternatives for financing your purchase of an existing business:

Use the seller's assets. As soon as you buy the business, you'll own the assets—so why not use them to get financing now? Make a list of all the assets you're buying (along with any attached liabilities), and use it to approach banks, finance companies, and factors (companies that buy accounts receivable).

Buy co-op. If you can't afford the business yourself, try going co-op—buying with someone else, that is. To find a likely co-op buyer, ask the seller for a list of people who were interested in the business but didn't have enough money to buy. (Be sure to have your lawyer write up a partnership agreement, including a buyout clause, before entering into any partnership arrangement.)

Use an Employee Stock Ownership Plan (ESOP). ESOPs offer you a way to get capital immediately by selling stock in the business to employees. If you sell only nonvoting shares of stock, you still retain control. By offering to set up an ESOP plan, you may be able to get a business for as little as 10 percent of the purchase price.

Lease with an option to buy. Some sellers will let you lease a business with an option to buy. You make a down payment, become a minority stockholder, and operate the business as if it were your own.

Six Common Mistakes to Avoid

1. **Being overanxious.** Don't be too anxious when you're looking to buy a business. If you're too anxious, this can affect the price. Anxiety and impatience aren't going to help you buy a business. Take your time. Recognize that there's always time to reflect on the business that's for sale. No matter what a business broker, a business seller, or any other person may tell you, there's always time. Nine times out of ten, the business that's up for sale is going to be around for a while. And if it's not, then it's the seller who is going to be the anxious one—and the seller's anxiety, of course, is something that can be manipulated to your advantage as a buyer.

2. **Buying on price alone.** Buyers often don't take ROI into account. If you're going to invest $20,000 in a business that returns a 5 percent net, you're better off putting your money in stocks and commodities, the local S&L, or municipal bonds.

Any type of intangible security is going to produce more than 5 percent.

3. **Having too little cash/misusing cash.** Some buyers use all their cash for the down payment on the business, even though having ample cash on hand for the start-up phase of any business, new or existing, is fundamental to short-term success. (Remember Alicia's and Marcia's experiences with the franchises.) They fail to predict future cash flow and possible contingencies that might require more capital. Further, there has to be some revenue set aside for building the business via marketing and PR efforts. So if you have $50,000 to invest, make sure you don't spend the entire amount on the purchase. Keep some of the capital. Remember all the franchise owners and business buyers mentioned in this chapter? They all stressed the importance of having a hefty stash of start-up capital. And they all said that no matter how much they thought they had, it was not enough. Though figures vary from industry to industry, a common contingency fund is 10 percent of the purchase price. You may also want to set aside enough to cover about three months' worth of expenses.

4. **Failing to double-check.** Most business buyers accept all the information and data given to them by the seller at face value, without the verification of their own accountant (preferably a CPA, who can audit financial statements).

5. **Agreeing to hefty payment schedules.** Novice business owners often overestimate their revenue during the first year and take on unduly large payments to finance the buyout. Those high revenue expectations rarely pan out. During the first year of any operation, the owner gets hit with unexpected costs such as equipment failures or employee turnover. That's why it makes more sense to have a payment schedule that begins fairly light,

then gets progressively heavier. This is something that can be negotiated with a seller and should not be difficult to arrange.

6. **Treating the seller unfairly.** People think that because they are buying a business, the seller is at their mercy. All too often, the buyer will be cold, rigid, and hardheaded, going for the sledgehammer approach. This isn't your best move. Just because you have some money and may be interested in purchasing the business, that doesn't mean that you aren't going to have to give a little in the process of negotiation. And it doesn't ever hurt to be nice.

These guidelines should give some general idea of whether buying a business or starting a franchise is an option for you. Whether you're starting an existing business or building yours from scratch, there are some pretty important skills that every business owner needs.

FROM FILM PRODUCTION
TO FOOD PRODUCTION

Karen Jackson, owner of Crunchy Foods, the umbrella company for Biscotti de Suzy, a gourmet bakery company Jackson purchased

For fifteen years Karen Jackson had a great career in the film industry. She was an award-winning producer on the hit Disney movie Toy Story 2 *and had a fabulous nine-year stint working at Pixar Animation Studios. As a producer on* Toy Story 2, *Jackson received a Golden Globe Award for Best Picture—Musical or Comedy. She was flying high.*

Today she deals with a different cast of characters as the owner of Crunchy Foods, which produces Biscotti de Suzy—the gourmet bakery line she purchased for $200,000 in the early 2000s. The Biscotti de Suzy line can be found nationwide at Marshalls and T. J. Maxx and at select Whole Foods in the San Francisco Bay area.

Initially, it was Karen's love for her babies, not biscotti, that led her to the crunchy treat. Like many women, motherhood caused Karen to rethink her priorities and her time commitment to her job. "I loved working for Pixar but I wanted to spend more time with my family. It was the classic situation where a working mother starts to understand how much she is missing," says the Los Angeles native and Stanford alum.

Karen left Pixar and took a few years off, staying home with her two boys. "But I needed to be challenged and fulfilled too. So I said, okay, what's next? Do I go back to the production world? Or do I want to do something on my own?

My husband and I talked about going into business together for years. We had complementary skills that we thought would work well together. I love the food industry and always wanted to own my own food company." Since she took the reins, the company has had double-digit revenue growth every year—that kind of success always goes down nicely.

Karen shares her tips for successfully buying a business:

Do the research

We worked our personal network and the Internet to see what types of businesses were out there. My husband is in banking, so he had connections with people who help others find business opportunities. I also started searching online and in the yellow pages for "business brokers" and doing searches for "businesses for sale." Look through the *Wall Street Journal*'s small-business website, online.wsj.com/small-business.

Create your own business entity to buy the business

Our plan was to form an LLC to create an umbrella business for the biscotti business and any other future food businesses we acquired.

Be ready to put your money where your mouth is

We had to put a few thousand dollars into an escrow account once our initial talks began to show that we were serious. We also had to show proof of assets and capital such that we could actually complete the deal.

Know what you're buying

Meet with the owners and talk to them as much as possible. We listened to their story and openly discussed why they were selling. Then we got to the real work. We thoroughly reviewed the books on site. They were not extremely professional records, mostly QuickBooks stuff, so we spent some extra time going through the records to make sure the actual financial history matched with what they were filing with the IRS and their own internal records. I also got the serial numbers for all the equipment that would be included in the purchase price and I researched how much it cost new along with its depreciation and current value. At the end of the process we knew exactly how much the hard assets were worth and how much goodwill value there was, as well as other tangible and intangible assets.

The company was marginally profitable, with just under $250,000 in annual sales over the years and three employees. The business had positive cash flow but had never earned more than $500,000 in sales, and revenues were decreasing when we came in. The previous owners saw the business more like a lifestyle venture and weren't necessarily interested in growing big. But we saw a lot of potential.

Get involved with the company

Spend as much time as possible watching and learning the business. I spent two months going into the store almost every day and helping with production; I watched the phone calls that were made, went on customer visits, and did other ride-alongs. I was favorably introduced to the major clients, and the previous owners stayed around during the transition to make sure those clients felt comfortable. The seller has to make those relationships continue when critical clients are involved. Consider having the seller stay on board as an employee, consultant, or other ongoing capacity. Also, I wasn't initially introduced to the employees as the new future owner but as someone who was coming in to help—that made them more receptive and open to my presence.

Negotiate smart

They asked for $300,000. We were thinking more like $200,000, which is where we ended up. We paid $150,000 up front and $50,000 over three years. We had a noncompete clause in our contract. And for three years they had to agree to consult with us. We also solicited a lot of advice from our network of savvy business folks and then did the actual negotiation ourselves.

Have a business plan and a team

We had a three- to five-year business plan that we created for the company. You also need to bring in outside advisers. Develop a board of directors who can give you informal advice or have other people who can help keep you focused and on track.

CHAPTER FIVE

Entrepreneurship 101: Eight Essential Business Skills for Success

You can't change a thing until you change your mind.
The real skill every entrepreneur needs is
the skill of receiving and allowing.
Acquire the skill of being willing.
—Andrew Morrison, business coach and founder of Small
Business Camp, New York www.90dayplan.com/

We've all seen it so many times before. What seems to be a great business opens up and then within months there's a "Going Out of Business" sign in the window. From a promising new restaurant or much-needed product to a service that you thought was ingenious—all gone before you could try it out. Grand opening! Grand closing! What happens to make good ideas crash and burn? In most cases, bad business management. Poor budgeting, no marketing plan, not knowing when or how to build the right team, poor strategic planning, yadda, yadda, yadda. The point is, great ideas can quickly turn into money pits and dashed dreams because of a lack of business savvy. Don't let that happen to you.

Now that you've got your fully focused kick-butt business idea backed by solid market research, determination, and a renewed self-confidence, it's time to brush up on your business skills so you have the tools to drive your business success. Many entrepreneurs are so focused on being creative and passionate, they overlook the importance of at least some basic business know-how, often to their detriment. Balance is key, my dear. Remember, an entrepreneur must wear several hats: marketing manager, finance manager, chief deal maker, public relations manager, and bookkeeper, to name a few. You don't necessarily need to have a marketing degree or an MBA or be a CPA to do all that, but you certainly need some basic skills. There are some skill sets you can hire but there are others that only you—as the vision leader and founder of the company—can and must bring to the table.

I've identified nine key skills that every entrepreneur needs to stay ahead of the game. In the early days when you're a one-woman show, it's imperative that you have at least a basic knowledge of and skill level in these key areas. They are Mocha Manual must-haves and will put you on the right path to starting, developing, financing, and marketing your business enterprise.

1. Sales and Marketing Skills

When I polled hundreds of entrepreneurs in the course of writing this book and asked them to name the most important business skills required for success, respondents overwhelmingly said marketing know-how was the number one skill needed. Ladies, if you can't sell it, nobody is going to buy it. And if nobody buys it, whether it's a good or a service, you are not in business. Sales and marketing are the two most important skills any business owner needs. You can have the most amazing, must-have product or boom-banging service, but if there aren't enough people who know about it to generate significant revenue, then you are not in business. Without customers and sales you have no business. And you won't have any sales without effective and aggressive marketing. You have to get out there and use whatever tools and avenues you can afford to generate buzz, target your audience, connect with your customers, and respond to their needs.

ACTION PLAN

You may need to brush up on your presentation and writing skills, as you'll need to talk to people and write ads, website copy, and press releases about your business. One of your best marketing tools is your mouth. Speaking about your business whenever you can, putting yourself out there to network, and approaching would-be clients on the street can be a great way to market yourself. For many of us, this is easier said than done. In general, women tend to have difficulty talking about themselves. Most of us aren't good at tooting our own horns because we're taught that good girls don't brag or that the Lord wants us to be humble. While boys grow up vying for the limelight and learning how to one-up each other, we are taught that good girls share the glory. We aren't supposed to be the center of attention. We blend in. We defer compliments. So often in the work world, we sit idly by, mad as hell, as we get passed over for promotions, high-visibility assignments, committee chairmanships, and so on because we don't draw attention to ourselves and our accomplishments. You don't have time for this when you're the boss and your income is dependent upon your own performance.

> **Tough Times Tip:** During a downturn, the marketing budget is usually the first item that gets cut. That's why it's important to be proactive in understanding what grassroots and online marketing efforts you can do on your own or with little outlay.

I used to act in the same way and I didn't even realize it. Anyone who knows me personally will vouch that I have a pretty strong personality. I'm very outgoing and have rarely walked into a room I couldn't work. But when it came time for me to get out there and market myself as the author of *The Mocha Manual to a Fabulous Pregnancy,* I realized I had issues. Under the expert media training of Taylor Made Media (www.taylormademediapr.com), I realized that I had trouble talking about myself and my accomplishments. I loved talking about the women in the book and the project, but when things got personal or when I was in a situation like, oh, I don't know, standing in front of a pregnant woman, it was hard for me to say something as basic as "Have you heard of my book, *The Mocha Manual to a Fabulous Pregnancy*?" At *Essence,* I rarely ever talked about my book. In an office full of black women! It was nuts. Karen of Taylor Made advised me (okay, told me) that I needed to start showcasing my accomplishments and talking about them. My first task was to put the lovely promotional card for my book into a frame and put it in my office. This was an indirect way for me to talk about *The Mocha Manual,* show people what I was doing, and hopefully take some of the pressure off me by allowing them to ask a question to start the conversation. I also started keeping my promo cards in my handbag and making it a personal goal to talk to at least one person a day about the book and my company.

Studies show that not only do women not draw attention to our accomplishments, we downplay them. Strangely enough, I didn't even like positive attention. As I started to delve into this surprising behavior, I had a breakthrough. (Well, my girlfriends told me off.) I was not-so-nicely informed that I always deflect compliments. If someone says to me, "You look nice," I usually respond with, "This old dress?" or "My hair is a mess," or something else to minimize the compliment. I started making a conscious effort to just say "thank you" when paid a compliment instead of jumping into my usual disclaimers.

Erin Braxton, who left a career in advertising, faced a similar challenge when launching her sleepwear and loungewear line. She had an amazing hustler spirit, but when it came time to get out there and sell her own designs, she flinched. "It intimidated me. It was a different kind of pressure because these were *my* designs. I had to work through that. Now I know I'm the best person to pitch my products," she says.

If you can learn the art of tasteful self-promotion and "work through" whatever is holding you back, you'll be a business superstar. Whether you are marketing a business, a service, or yourself, you have to get out there, generate buzz, and network (see more specific tips and ideas in chapter 5).

2. Money Management Skills

You may know your business, but you also need to know the numbers behind your business in order to be successful. Now, if you have no desire to make money, please close this book now. The rest of us are in business to make money. In order to make money you have to be able to handle money well. I'm sure you've heard of high-earning businesses that fell by the wayside because of silly spending. Hey, it happened to most of the high-flying Internet companies in the '90s that had $100 million in funding but blew it on expensive jets, lavish trips, and generally living fat, only to have their money run out in a year. So it could happen to you. Don't go there. You gotta learn how to budget, how to manage spending so no money is wasted, and how to figure out the best pricing structure for your good or service.

If you are able to manage your cash flow well when the business starts to run, you will be able to survive the ups and downs of self-employment. The important thing is to always focus on the bottom line. For every expenditure, always ask yourself: "How much will this contribute to my bottom line?" If it will not give your business anything in return financially, better think twice before writing that company check.

ACTION PLAN

The reality is that you will never understand your business until you understand its finances—how it makes money, how it spends money, where it gets money, what its cash cycles are. I know you barely have enough time in the day as it is, but you really can't afford *not* to take the time to look at your business finances. Remember, knowledge is power. Just as you're knowledgeable about your products or services and have confidence in your abilities, you can be equally empowered when it comes to your company's finances. Sometimes that power comes from knowing when to ask for help or hire a professional. But even Oprah will tell you, never let anyone have complete financial control over your business. Now, if Oprah is not willing to lose any of her billions, I'm sure you can't afford to mismanage your stash—which I'm guessing is considerably less.

There's an old cliché in management circles that I picked up during all those years at *Fortune* magazine. The saying is "If you can't measure something, you can't manage it." Things need to be quantifiable—that means you need to put a number to them, a dollar figure, percentage, sumthin'! I've asked a lot of impressive entrepreneurs how much it costs to produce their product or service and they often rattle off a lot of stuff, but it's all preceded by "about." Most likely, they don't have a real idea of the true cost of their products or services. At one point, I was in the same boat. When I started producing the maternity shirts, I used a manufacturer in India because the price of the shirt was much cheaper than the prices I received from American manufacturers. I thought I was doing good! I figured that even with the shipping costs I was coming out ahead. I struggled on, dealing with disappointments from overseas, staying up until ungodly hours to communicate with India, and getting faulty goods for a while, thinking it was worth the cheaper cost. After I got burned and stiffed for a few thousand dollars I really couldn't afford to waste, I sat down with a pen, paper, and calculator. When I figured out the actual cost (not just an in-my-head estimation) of each shirt, including shipping, customs agent fees, and then my shirt printing costs, I realized that some of the American manufacturers weren't that expensive after all. And then the price for peace of mind, not living on New Delhi time, and the comfort of knowing that if something got ugly I could jump on a plane and go to the factory was well worth the few extra dollars. Point is, until I measured it, I couldn't manage it properly. When you can track money going through your company, you have a powerful tool for making decisions such as:

- Is this product/service profitable? Does it meet my minimum standards?
- Is this customer profitable? Does he or she meet my minimum standards?
- Which of these new products/services should we attempt? Why? Why not?
- What is the best use of my assets/funds?

To avoid guesstimating at any of these questions, you need to manage your expenses and income properly by writing it down and tracking it. Thankfully, this no longer involves dreadful ledger books with debit and credit columns and daunting green lines. Remember those? Today there is a lot of savvy software to help you stay on top of your game. Investing in easy-to-use accounting software like QuickBooks or Quicken Basic is money well spent. You can also contact a local Small Business Administration (SBA) or Small Business Development Corp. (SBDC) office for assistance (see appendix). You can find low-cost or free accounting seminars online or in your area by contacting your local community college, SBA office, or SBDC office (see appendix).

If you ever need to present your company to people who lend money, approve leases, or okay any other financial arrangements, you will need to have three key financial reports about your business: the balance sheet, the income statement, and a statement of cash flow. Each of these tells a different story about your business. The balance sheet, which lists assets and liabilities, is a snapshot of how healthy your company is at a particular point in time. The income statement tells you if your company is making a profit or losing money during a specific period of time. And the statement of cash flow explains any increase or decrease in cash on the balance sheet and follows the cash flow in your business. When you get familiar with these documents, you'll have your finger on the pulse of your company's finances.

3. Self-Motivation Skills

Let's face it, toots, you're on your own out there. Nobody is going to make it happen but you. There's no time clock to punch, no boss breathing down your neck, no painful quarterly employee evaluations to compel you to do your job. Everything falls on your shoulder pads. To win at the entrepreneur game, you have to be a self-starter with a clear goal in mind. You need confidence in yourself and your ideas. But even the sister with the strongest swagger can fall into a motivational slump every now and then. Especially if you work at home, it is doubly hard to get into the work mind-set: sometimes, the television is just so tempting that it's hard to get out of your pajamas and begin typing on your computer. You therefore must have that extra drive and commitment to realite sure that you are taking the necessary steps to realize your dream of a successful business.

While your passion can drive you to new heights, the truth is, some of the mundane administrative tasks can drive you to drink. Dealing with difficult customers or clients, invoices, vendors, and sales slumps can really test and drain your motivation. It also steals away time from being creative and thinking big. You need to effectively manage those tasks so that they are not energy wasters and time wasters.

ACTION PLAN

To keep yourself motivated, think about why you started on this journey in the first place. As acting coaches ask their students, "What's your motivation?" To stay connected to your drive and get big dreaming back in effect, schedule time for a weekly "meeting of one." This is your time to let your passion infuse your big-picture thinking and come up with new ideas to take your business to the next level.

Find your own ways to stay motivated. Why are you doing this? Sometimes you can be money motivated. There is a mortgage to be paid, so sales goals need to be met, plain and simple. That's very real. For others, it's more important to focus on what they give their customers, what they are contributing to the world, and how they are making a difference. Perhaps the Bible can be your source of motivation. Either way, learn to focus on the positive, particularly as you start your day. Begin with a daily affirmation or your personal mantra for getting rich, being fabulous, or taking over the world! Surround your work space with words, quotes, pictures, and photographs that help you stay inspired. Find your inspiration from all sorts of places. On my wall there are quotes from Shakespeare and Benjamin Franklin; "Our Deepest Fear," a poem by Marianne Williamson; and a li'l sumthin' sumthin' from Jay-Z.

Karen Taylor Bass of Taylor Made Media put me on to dream boards. She's been keeping one for years, and depending on where she was in her life, it has included pictures of cars, homes, and more recently, a baby. By actually visualizing her ideal life, she's accomplished everything the dream board held, down to her precious baby girl, Sofia. The board just keeps changing and evolving to suit where she is in her life and her business.

There may be people in your life who can help you stay motivated. Karen always gets inspired by her grandmother. "With just a fifth-grade education she has been able to buy and sell real estate many times. She cleaned people's asses in a hospital for years. But she never believed in credit. She always said if you can't buy it twice then you don't need it. She bought her first house with cash. They stayed on one floor and rented the rest. Then she sold it, moved to Florida, and built three homes. If Grandma can do all of that with a fifth-grade education, there is no excuse for me." Practice recalling the experience of the matriarchs and patriarchs of your family. Think about what they survived and their ability to keep on keepin' on and you'll find your motivation too.

You also need to surround yourself with like-minded people. Join a group for entrepreneurs locally or even online. If you're hanging around a group of nine-to-fivers who don't necessarily have the entrepreneurial bug, it may be hard to stay motivated. But when you're around others who share your life plan, you'll find yourself energized and buzzing with excitement. Trust me!

If motivation still doesn't come easy, think about getting a business coach or at least a business buddy. Over the years, I've had informal buddy arrangements with a few girlfriends and acquaintances, old and new. As we were building our respective businesses, we checked in with each other every week to hear about recent developments and upcoming plans. Sometimes we just helped each other stay focused or served as a listening ear or shoulder to cry on. Either way, it's invaluable to have someone in your corner who understands the vicissitudes of an entrepreneur's life and who can help you dust off and get back in the game.

4. Time Management Skills

If you can't manage your time, you'll never get anything done. And entrepreneurs need to get stuff done all day, every day. When you're a one-woman show you don't have the luxury of wasting time. By the time you blink twice when you wake up, you should have a clear idea of the things you need to do for the day. You must have the ability to multitask. In a typical day, you will be the secretary in the morning, typing all correspondence and e-mails; become the marketing pro writing press releases before noon; make sales calls in the afternoon; and become a book-keeper before your closing hours. If you sell products, you may still have to create the products, deliver and fulfill the orders, rush to the bank to cash the checks. Sounds like a day for Super-woman. But you will be able to do it all (although sometimes not all in one day) if you master the skills of managing time and learn how to properly prioritize your tasks.

ACTION PLAN

The secret sauce to great time management is eliminating time wasters. One of the biggest causes of wasted time is procrastina-tion. All you procrastinators out there, you know who you are! Yes, I'm talking to you, Ms. I'll Do It Tomorrow. When you learn to recognize the warning signs of procrastination, then you can help stop the madness. What kind of procrastinator are you? This is not to say that you're not a hard worker. In fact, procras-tinators often work as many hours in a day as anyone else, some-times even more. The problem is that they often invest their time in all the wrong tasks. Sometimes they simply just do not under-stand the difference between urgent tasks and important ones.

Or they are always waiting for the "right" mood or the "right" time to take on a task. Sometimes the procrastination is rooted in a fear of failure or success or some sick sense of perfectionism ("I can't do it perfectly so I won't do it at all"). No matter where it comes from, it can really ruin your chances of business success.

For years, Suzanne Bishopson, a thirty-six-year-old mother of two in Commack, New York, could not get her IT consulting business off the ground. "I would spend hours trying to get things done and I always felt like I was spinning my wheels," she says. Suzanne thought she had all the right moves—she was making long lists of all the things she had to do, then starting early, staying up late, and putting in many hours. Despite her best efforts, Suzanne was missing a key component of the time-management game. Sure, she had a to-do list, but it was structured all wrong. The trick to mastering the art of the to-do list is to have not one but two, three, or sometimes four versions of the list. Here's how to be checklist savvy. Start by writing down all the tasks you have to do. If there are biggies, break them down into smaller pieces. If any items still seem large, break them down again. Do this until you have listed everything you have to do and until each task will take no more than one to two hours to complete.

Okay. You're almost a real diva of to-do lists. The next step is to review your list, this time giving every task a priority status using numbers or letters. For example, A would be very important and F would be unimportant. If too many tasks have a high priority, go through the list yet again and demote the less important ones. Once you have done this, rewrite the list in priority order and voilà! You've got a superefficient list to help you take on your day.

You can use this process differently depending on what type

of business you have and the type of tasks you have on your plate. If you are in a sales-type role, a good way of motivating yourself is to keep your list relatively short and aim to complete it every day. If you're in more of an operational role, or if tasks are large or dependent on too many other people, then it may be better to keep one list and chip away at it every day.

You may find that some unimportant jobs get moved from one to-do list to the next. Or you may not be able to complete some very low-priority jobs for several months. Don't worry about this unless you have a deadline to meet. If so, raise their priority pronto. When you become an ace at producing prioritized to-do lists, you'll become amazingly productive and efficient.

Now, it's one thing to have a great list, but you also need to know how to properly structure your day to make sure you knock out as much of that list as possible. This is where Suzanne was able to make the biggest strides in improving her productivity. How many times did you have a killer list and lots of energy for taking it on, only to unintentionally spend way too much time answering e-mails or making phone calls? Answering e-mails is my biggest drain. I start out by setting aside uninterrupted time for a particular task, but then my Outlook starts to ding and my curiosity about who it is gets the better of me. It's an alluring sound—or maybe I'm just looking for a reason to take a break. Who knows? Either way, you start with one and the next thing you know, you've lost an hour or more. The same is true of answering the phone or returning calls. Karen Taylor Bass found that when she answered the phones, she started chatting or the person she was calling began chatting, and the next thing she knew she was on the phone for twenty or thirty minutes for what should have been a five-minute call. Another time stealer. When you've got a nine-to-five job, children, or other family responsibilities and a lot to get done, an hour is precious time not to be wasted. Karen decided to hire someone to answer phones; this freed her to focus on the big-picture tasks and being creative. To avoid the e-mail trap, phone-answering trap, or any other time stealer, think of your day in building blocks.

Large Blocks: Your Day's Foundation

The foundation of your day should be an uninterrupted block of time where you can focus on difficult, involved projects. These should be from the high-priority section of your to-do list. Ideally, you should block out an hour and a half, or approximately 20 percent of an eight-hour day. If you can't squeeze out that much time, try for at least an hour. Even with forty-five minutes of uninterrupted time you can get a lot of work done because you won't waste a moment. I used to say one hour, only to lift my head two hours later, cursing myself. Now, I set my BlackBerry or Outlook alarm to ring when my allotted time is up. And when I'm in the "do not disturb" zone, I start by turning off my e-mail notification (that darn ding is sooo inviting), and then I turn off the phone ringer. If you want to make sure that a certain person or e-mail message gets through immediately, you can set up your e-mail to notify you of that specific message. When you can block off 20 percent of your time to focus on what's really important, you'll be sure to accomplish about 80 percent of your work for the day.

Then you have your medium blocks. Now, I know you're a multitasking phenom, but some studies suggest that isn't the most productive mode. According to one report, you are four times more productive when you can focus on one type of task rather than switching among varied tasks. In other words, multitasking slows you down. Instead, try grouping similar activities together as much as possible, such as returning nonurgent phone calls, answering e-mail, filing, or other administrative stuff. How long you spend on like tasks depends on the type of work you'll be doing. For example, if you just need to return five short phone calls, you may only need to block out ten to fifteen minutes to do that. You may need a half hour for answering e-mails. The beauty is, you can even repeat these blocks during the day. For instance, I like to spend ten minutes checking my e-mail first thing in the morning to take care of any pressing issues, then another thirty minutes right before my lunch break and another thirty minutes later on in the afternoon. But if you allot thirty minutes, you have to stick to thirty minutes. That will help keep you focused on what you're working on at that time and boost your productivity. Since these blocks work like interchangeable parts, move any tasks you don't complete to the next block of time.

You structure your day by finding space for that large block, followed by several medium blocks of grouped activities. What's left are the small blocks of time that represent the lower-priority tasks and any new items. These fill in the gaps of your day and can include stuff like quick research, ordering supplies, online banking, and other project components that didn't fit into your major blocks but are still necessary.

I used to do the opposite, thinking that if I took care of the small things first I could fully focus on my big tasks. But I ended up bogged down in the small items, without finding time for my most important work. My day would fly by with no real movement on my priorities. Learning better time management transformed my productivity and my business results.

5. Administration Skills

Managing all the paperwork of a business, even if most of it is now done electronically, is still a major pain in the butt. You need to file your receipts properly, get your sales tax in on time, and keep other corporate filings up to date so that tax time won't be Chinese torture and you won't get hit with costly fees and penalties (been there, done that!). You also need to do all the work in terms of billing, printing invoices, collecting payments, and managing your receivables. That means you need to organize your office space, file your papers properly, and stay on top of your bills. This is a good time to start buddying up to any friends or family members who may have a responsible college student among their ranks. You may be able to hire a college student or local stay-at-home mom who is looking for a few hours' work for extra cash. I found great office help by offering myself as the world's best mentor to students in the journalism school at a nearby university. I got some administrative help for a few hours a week in return for career advice, advising on a few papers, and helping with a few job applications. Win-win!

Before you can get anyone to help, you need an easy-to-follow organization system. Basic paperwork like customer invoices, purchase orders, shipping receipts, expense receipts, etc. need to have a home—and shoe boxes aren't really what I'm talking about here. Having an effective system will minimize errors due to misplacement, make it easier for anyone who is helping you to get things done, and decrease the amount of time spent handling paper.

ACTION PLAN

I have to admit that most of my experience here will come from the "what not to do" category. This is one of those areas where I have recognized my weakness and sacrificed lunches out or new shoes to pay for the help of an able office assistant. To be honest, I have a long history of messy offices. I used to call it my "highly specialized filing system that only I can understand," but the truth was I couldn't find a darn thing. This really wrecked my flow and my ability to get things done quickly both at my job and in my business. The good news for you and me is that organization is a skill that can be learned. Some of my favorite assistants, like Veronica and Tamika, have taught me invaluable lessons along the way, but admittedly, I'm still a work in progress. So I'll share a few tips that I've learned and some from organization experts. The trick is to break old habits, like letting papers pile up (guilty!) and writing important notes on random pieces of paper like envelopes and napkins (guilty again!). But enough about me; let's get started.

Tip #1: **Do as much as you can online. You can find great software or Internet websites to manage invoices, pay bills, and track other business records. The more you can file and handle electronically, the better. Just make sure you have a backup on an external hard drive or even paper.**

Tip #2: **Make it a rule to always refile things. This was one of Tamika's biggest rules. You can create a special place, like a desktop standing file, for current projects, but otherwise put everything away.**

Tip #3: Put loose papers in labeled folders (such as "To Do" or "For Review") or use a color-coded system—green files for invoices, red for legal matters, etc.

Tip #4: Use a planner, electronic or paper. This is one area where I have really learned to shine. I put appointments, due dates, notes, and important details in my PDA immediately. Whether you are typing with your thumbs on a Treo or BlackBerry or writing in a planner, both are great places to record ideas in development, a new marketing idea, a clever slogan, anecdotes, or details of a phone conversation. Whatever it is, put it in one key place and then you won't have scraps of paper all over with no idea of where to find them.

Tip #5: Spend some time every day clearing off your desk. When you start creating the time blocks of your day, include uninterrupted time (that means no phone, no e-mail) for tidying your desk and filing paperwork. Remember, getting organized is the first step, but you'll need persistence and follow-through to keep you that way.

6. Networking Know-How

You'll be hard pressed to find anyone who won't shout at the top of their lungs about the power of networking. Nothing beats personal connections, a referral, and expanding your Rolodex of contacts in your industry. There are two levels of networking. There's your personal network, and there are the trade shows and industry events you attend to build your industry network. Every woman I interviewed as part of the research for this book said that networking was an invaluable skill that saved their bacon many times. It is the lifeblood of any business. Many black women have a personality advantage in the networking game; we tend to be social creatures and somewhat outgoing. [Plus, most of us have learned to master the real game—the white people game.] Whether with coworkers, school friends, or neighbors, we have a unique experience with fitting in, understanding what makes someone tick, and establishing some common ground. These are all valuable assets in playing the networking game. Let's be clear: networking is not socializing. There is a social aspect to networking, but networking is results oriented, whether directly (I want something from you now!) or indirectly (I may want something from you later). There are strategies to execute, rules of engagement, and goals to be met, or else you're just making calls and hanging out.

ACTION PLAN

Before we can get into action, there may be some of you who are battling shyness, a lack of confidence, or something else that impedes your networking power. The first thing to remember is that you do have power, and your business needs you to unleash it and harness it for your personal and business success. More good news—research shows that shyness is a learned behavior that can actually be unlearned. As a child you may wander over to someone at a play area, introduce yourself, and play. No problem! But as we get older, we experience rejection—which doesn't feel so good—so we shy away from being friendly. If shyness is a challenge for you, start by striking up a conversation with a stranger in the elevator just before you have to get off. Try saying something quick and easy, like "Have a nice day," or "Great shoes."

The rest of your action plan involves using the following strategies:

1. **Focus on quality vs. quantity**—The number of people you know does not matter. It is the quality of your contacts that does. Who are the decision makers? The influencers? Who can you help and how? Make sure your efforts lead to quality contacts.

2. **Slow down**—Building business relationships take time. Get to know people not only from a business perspective but from a personal perspective too.

3. **Go low-tech**—In some cases, a quick phone call can be more efficient than many e-mails. Pick up the phone and even find time to meet face-to-face. E-mail is excellent when sending documents or directions, but don't overuse it.

4. **Seek diversity**—Make sure you have a diverse network of connections.

5. **Appreciate introductions**—When someone takes time out of his or her day to make the effort to introduce you, it is the ultimate flattery. This separates name droppers from the genuine networkers.

6. **Practice third-party networking**—Take the time to introduce two people so they can benefit from meeting each other. You get to reconnect with someone when you don't need anything and become a "networking node."

7. **Go Zen**—Make this the year where you surround yourself with positive people who add value to you and your network while keeping your distance from those who distract and de-energize you.

8. **Avoid 911 networking**—Don't call someone just because you're in desperate need of referrals or leads. Build relationships *before* you need them.

9. **Make random "hello" calls**—When someone comes up in a conversation or comes to mind, make a random "hello" call. You don't need to have an agenda or reason; simply share that he or she was in your thoughts and you wanted to connect.

When you're out at a networking event:

1. Set a goal for yourself for how many new people you want to meet. Every time you go out, stretch your last goal, try to beat your last number, and push yourself a little harder.

2. A great way to network is to introduce yourself to someone who is standing alone.

3. People like to talk about themselves. It's not all about you, my dear. Ask them something about who they are, what they do, who they know, or what they hate about these kinds of parties.

4. Always ask for a business card. This helps you remember their names, you have a record of who they are and their contact info, and the back of a business card makes a great place to jot down any memorable things you learned or spoke about.

5. Remember, you are on a mission. When you're about to start or are already in a conversation, decide on the specific questions you would like to ask. Before the conversation ends, decide on a good next step for both of you (meet up, grab a bite, arrange a phone call, etc.). When you're talking to someone, be completely present with them and give them your undivided attention.

FOUR CONVERSATION STOPPERS
(AND HOW TO OVERCOME THEM)

Problem: I'm bored stiff. I can't think of anything else to say.

What to do: When the conversation lulls, move on—"Excuse me, there's someone I want to meet" is a perfectly acceptable thing to say. Smile and then walk away.

Problem: I'm looking silly with nothing to do.

What to do: Check your meet goals for the night and see how you're doing.

Problem: I know this person but I can't recall their name to save my life. What to do: Simply say, "Hello again. Please, remind me of your name." Then remind them of your name.

Problem: I'm stuck talking to a real jerk.

What to do: Ask if they've met anyone especially interesting that you might like to meet. Or point out someone you found interesting. Or both. And then move on.

---

7. Team Building

I know you like to do that Superwoman thing. Or better yet, you think that if you don't do it, it won't be done correctly. Or worse, perfectly! Gasp! This is another area where I am guilty as charged. But to build a company that grows and grows, you need to start building a team around you. That means collecting professionals and others who can support what you're doing in the business with either professional skills or personal support, or by serving in an advisory capacity. Every success story has a strong team. They say behind every successful man is a good woman. Well, behind every successful woman is a team of supporters, both professional and personal, who help propel her to the top. If you think you can make it on your own, I'm here—along with all the other entrepreneurs surveyed for this book—to tell you to get rid of that type of thinking ASAP. Now, supporters generally come in two forms: advisers and specialists. Some you hire, some you pay for, and some you obtain through networking and outreach. Obviously, you want to obtain your team as inexpensively as possible, but don't be afraid to pay for experience and expertise if necessary. Smart people at your side can save you years of hard work—and missteps.

> **Tough Times Tip:** When the economy is causing layoffs, a lot of highly qualified employees are out of work. This can be a great opportunity for small-business owners to find talented administrative, marketing, or advertising professionals who may have been otherwise out of their price range or unavailable. After being screwed by the corporate world they are also likely to be looking for more personally fulfilling work.

ACTION PLAN

When should you begin looking for these valued individuals? As soon as you're in business, especially if you're new to the process. There are some basic professional services every business should have. These include an accountant, an insurance agent, a lawyer, and a banker. They should also include a professional business coach, business mentor, or expert to get an accurate read on the validity and requirements of your future plans.

To get started, make a list of everyone you've ever known or met personally who might be of assistance. Relatives, old college friends, sorority sisters, church members old and new, and even friends of friends may have the perspective you need. Remember, objectivity is personality based, not relationship based. If a person is mature, experienced, and knowledgeable, they can be of value to you.

Now the idea of building a team is to actually let them do their work. Team building and delegating are signs of a good and effective leader. Instead of tiring yourself out wearing twelve hats, hand off two or three and free yourself up to be more creative or focus on what you love. A good leader knows her strengths and weaknesses. That means getting other people to do what they are good at while freeing yourself up to focus on your strengths. You're probably still busy thinking, *Nobody can do it like I can.* Sounds more like someone is afraid of losing control. It's important to realize that you don't lose control of a task just because someone else is doing it. You still have the final say. *It will cost me money* is another common excuse not to delegate. It may or may not. Delegating will certainly cost you some time, because you'll have to research the best provider for the task you seek to delegate.

As you begin to hire professionals in a specific discipline, however, don't automatically reach out for people you've retained in the past for other tasks. Just because your personal accountant does a great job on your tax return, for example, doesn't mean he or she will be the kind of bookkeeper that will benefit your company. I learned this lesson firsthand. My personal accountant was a great guy. I absolutely adored him and actually looked forward to our annual meeting to go over my taxes. But he wasn't experienced in corporate taxes. And I was holding on to him because of our personal relationship, while I was racking up penalties and fees for unpaid sales tax because he didn't really know much about business accounting. Personal relationships are important, but they should not come before the best interests of your business.

Look for people with proven experience working with businesses in your industry or with companies of similar size. In the early days of a business, every penny counts. You're right to manage costs and not add people until you absolutely have to, even if you have the cash reserves to support the payroll. However, the most expensive advice of all is free advice from a poor source. Get great advice and great help, even if you have to pay for it. It'll be worth it! Here are some questions to ask before hiring key professionals:

1. What is your experience in the field?
2. Have you handled matters like mine?
3. What are your rates and how often will you bill me?
4. What is a ballpark figure for the total bill, including fees and expenses?
5. What kind of approach will you take to resolve the matter—aggressive and unyielding, or will you be more inclined to reach a reasonable settlement?
6. Who else in your office may be responsible for my case?
7. Can you provide references?

8. Operations and Production

Business operations are the processes involved in creating value for your company. How does your business operate? How will you create value? What processes will you use? Without a process there is chaos, and when there is chaos there will be little business success. There has to be someone in charge of keeping the business functioning on a day-to-day basis and planning for the future. That's what you, as the CEO, must do. You make sure the business objectives are met.

In the world of operation gurus, the people who get paid big bucks by major corporations to manage operations, there's a language of inputs and outputs. Let's first consider the inputs. You may need to source required raw materials, finished products, or other supplies. Whether you are purchasing meat to put in a sandwich or clothing to hang in a retail store, you will be involved with manufacturers and distributors individually or through a larger-scale trade show or convention. Building supplier relationships and negotiating contracts are two of the initial steps you will need to take to build your operations.

As you use these inputs to generate outputs such as sales revenue and profits, there are many processes along the way that must be managed effectively. Whether your company makes a product or performs a service, someone in the organization should be able to plan and schedule the operations, project demand, monitor costs, establish appropriate controls, and create efficiencies where possible. That means you or someone you empower has to be planning, organizing, directing, and controlling matters to get that done.

Planning involves figuring out the right objectives for the business and how those objectives are going to be accomplished. This is one of the most commonly skipped steps in running a small business, yet it is also the one thing that can get you on track and keep you there. Make time for this step. Organizing means you get the resources and activities of the business aligned with meeting those objectives. This includes getting the right people to take care of the activities of the business, training them, and rewarding them appropriately. Remember, you are part of the human resources of your firm too and your needs need to be met also. So if you need health insurance, you should get some (see appendix). Directing is not just for Hollywood. You need to lead this business production. Know when to yell *Cut!* Know when to call *Action!* And know how to keep all the players (employees and others) motivated and on task to reach your goals. Learning how to lead is part skill, part art—some people are natural leaders but there are also skills you can learn to make yourself better at it. You have to abandon your need to be nice, learn how to communicate directions effectively, and learn how to correct and, if necessary, fire people who don't make the cut. In my early days as a manager, I would redo people's work instead of telling them that it wasn't good enough and they had to do it over. I thought I was saving time by doing it myself. But I actually did my team a disservice when I didn't give them honest, constructive feedback on their work. How will they get better if I don't point out weak areas?

An effective leader also knows how to control matters. That also comes under the "controlling" part of leadership. It's the process of evaluating and correcting to keep things on track. Planning and controlling are closely linked to each other, since planning sets the goals and standards for performance, and controlling checks to make certain the plan is being followed. It also gives an opportunity for feedback just in case the plan needs to be revised. And it means that sometimes certain people may have to be let go. In fact, business coach and serial entrepreneur Andrew Morrison says he always fires people as he hires them, as in, "I'll give you ninety days to meet this goal," or "Let's start with a thirty-day trial"; that way there's an understanding that your continued employment is based on performance. It also sets up a predetermined control mechanism—at the end of ninety or thirty days this relationship will be reevaluated.

In one of the entrepreneurship classes I took, we were schooled on the importance of an employee manual—not necessarily because anyone in the course had enough employees to merit a manual, but because there's a value in writing down how things are done in your business. From how calls are answered to how products are assembled and shipped, you need a process—a way of doing business. If you don't have one, you won't have an efficient operation. When you can learn to create a process, you master the role of operations and production. And your business can run efficiently in your absence.

Monique Greenwood, former editor in chief of *Essence* and the owner of the Akwaaba chain of bed-and-breakfasts, learned this firsthand. After playing innkeeper, cook, housekeeper, reservations manager, and more, she decided it was time to increase her staff. Especially since she couldn't be in all four inns at the same time. But she wanted to make sure the experience was the same for each visitor regardless of which inn they visited and regardless of whether she was there with her personal touches. Monique set about creating an operation manual covering everything, including how the beds should be made, how breakfast should be served, how reservations are booked, and even how the house lemonade is prepared. Monique is quick to admit that it was tough work (read more about Monique Greenwood's journey in entrepreneurship on pages 186–190), but well worth the effort. Now she can rest easy knowing that every inn has her signature service, whether she is there or not.

ACTION PLAN

When you go through the process of mapping out your operations, you are essentially creating the bible of how your business should be run. You decide exactly what's required in each area to perform the necessary functions. Then you write it down. When your operations manual is complete, you are free to spend time doing other things while you hand over your manual and watch your business continue to run according to your policies, procedures, and instructions. Start by answering these eight questions. Your end product should be simple enough for a child to understand and follow.

1. **What products/services do I sell?** Make a list of every product or service you offer. Figure out the exact cost of each product, including everything from raw product to finished goods to delivery. Make a list of every step required to actually get the supplies, make the product, and ship/deliver the product. Think like you're writing out a recipe with detailed step-by-step instructions.

2. **Whom do I sell to?** This part would cover your ideal target customer. Include a demographic profile, something about their lifestyle and personality traits, benefits they receive from buying from you, along with their wants, needs, and expectations in buying from you. All of this will help you develop a complete customer profile, which is important for anyone in your business who deals with customers.

3. **Who's in charge of selling the products?** This part covers the people who interact with your customers. What should they say? What's your best method for turning prospects into clients or customers? This could also include information on any sales training.

4. **How do you sell your product?** This should cover the full gamut, including marketing, advertising, actually getting customers, and making the sale. This will include a marketing plan with your core marketing message and unique selling position.

5. **What are the prices and terms?** Determine your retail pricing. Also consider any special, volume discount, or other promotional prices. What about wholesale prices? How much of a discount are you willing to offer to secure a client?

6. **How is the product produced?** Fully detail the production process from start to finish. Imagine you are going away and someone needs to follow the process exactly in your absence.

7. **How is it delivered?** Write out every step of how your end product gets into your customers' hands. How long should each step take?

8. **How is the product repaired, serviced, or replaced?** Set up a process to deal with damages, repairs, and dissatisfied customers. What is your return policy?

Standardizing your processes is a huge task, but when you can sleep easy knowing your business is running smoothly while you're off doing other things (maybe even relaxing!), it is a sweet reward.

Bonus Point: Plan B-Ability

This is not so much a skill as it is a mind-set that needs to be acquired. It sounds like plain ol' common sense but a sister has got to be flexible! Listen, even superheroes have backup plans. If Batman gets in a bind, Robin can swoop in and save his bacon.

Whatever phase of your business you are in, always have a backup plan, a plan B, and a plan C, D, and E if you're really smart.

This comes in particularly handy if your industry or the industry you serve has a change in fortunes. When you can adapt to economic downturns, upturns, and changes in consumer spending patterns, you will greatly boost your chances of business success.

When I sat down to interview Monique Greenwood, I absolutely loved how she talked about her inability to fail. This wasn't cockiness or bravado; she simply had so many contingency plans for each property, she knew that if one didn't work she could just transition into plan B and then C and so on and so on, until success happened. When you build a contingency plan into your actual planning, there is no failure; it's simply part of the plan! Fabulous!

Mocha Mix
My Most Valuable Business Skill

✳ ✳ ✳ ✳ ✳ ✳ ✳ ✳ ✳ ✳ ✳ ✳ ✳ ✳ ✳ ✳ ✳

Education can be an important foundation, but practical experience is even more important. You learn the best lessons from practicing your profession.
— AQUILA BARNES, founder of Shene Productions, a postproduction house in New York

Nothing beats knowing how to properly develop and use relationships. Follow-through is very important. We are often not taught these things.
— JINNIE ENGLISH, president of Chicago's High Achievers, Illinois (www.getting-better.net)

Writing is an important business skill. Whether it's your website copy, marketing materials, proposals, or press releases, good writing is essential. Well-written press releases build impressions and establish credibility.
— DOREEN MOTTON, CEO of Neero & Ana, New York (www.neero-ana.net)

You really need to be polished and know how to clearly communicate and present your ideas.
— MAYAI CHATMAN, CEO of Wedding Day, Inc., a wedding consulting firm in New York (www.wednday.com)

Women can easily get caught in the weeds—the day-to-day of running the business—and miss out on all-important networking. Get out there and get attached. Get a network.

— GINA STERN, owner of D_parture Spa (www.departure spa.com)

Educating yourself on finance, accounting, and marketing is important. You also need the ability to communicate effectively and a certain level of confidence.

— TRICIALEE RILEY, owner of Polish Bar of Brooklyn, New York (www.polishbarbrooklyn.com)

Having solid project-management skills allows me to take on varied clients. It also helps me understand what upper management wants to see and how to simplify what can be a very technical process.

— NQUAVAH JAMES, founder of All Things Post, LLC, a postproduction house in New York

FROM HIGH SCHOOL DROPOUT
TO TERMINAL TAKEOFF

Gina Stern, owner of D_parture Spa, an in-terminal full-service salon, with two locations at Newark Airport in New Jersey and one at Orlando International Airport in Florida

Gina Stern really knows how to fly. After all, she pioneered the airport spa concept, then was relentless in convincing airport management to give prime retail space to a young woman from the Bronx who was raised on welfare and then dropped out of high school in the eleventh grade. She had an unproven business idea, no spa experience, and a big dream.

But what Gina may have lacked in experience she made up for with hard-charging drive and an uncanny human depth. Drawing from her own negative airport experiences, Gina saw her business as a conduit of change for others, taking them from the experience they were having to the experience they wanted to have. "I remember being stuck in the airport for several hours thinking there had to be a better way for the traveler," she says.

So did everyone else. Gina foresaw time as the new currency. "People are time-poor and weary. I saw time being disrespected and offered a way to do the things you want to do at the airport," she says. And in solving that problem at the airport, Gina found a million-dollar business idea.

Business took off. D_parture Spa, which offers manicures, pedicures, haircuts, hair coloring, waxing, facials, and massage along with travel-sized grooming products, even earplugs and relaxing eye masks, earned half a million dollars in revenues in its first nine months in business. Then 9/11 hit and nearly destroyed Gina's revenues and her fighting spirit. Five years and many lessons learned later, she soared back to the top. D_parture Spa surpassed a million dollars in revenue in 2006 and hasn't looked back. Hilary Swank, Nelly Furtado, and Patrick Kennedy are some of the reported celebrity clients. Today, the sky's the limit.

Gina shares her secrets for a successful liftoff:

You first

The first business enterprise is you. If you have a big concept, investors are betting on you. How you deal with adversity and setbacks in your personal life is how you will deal with them in your business. Before you start a business, be clear about how you're dealing with yourself.

After getting my GED and working in retail for several years, I had a breakthrough at age twenty-five. I felt inadequate with my life. I saw myself constantly giving up my power and I wanted to do something about it. I decided to go to college and study fashion. Despite my past school experiences, I made the dean's list and became the first college graduate in my family. I needed to do that.

Turn life's lemons into lemonade

I was doing very well in the fashion industry. Then, one day, I fell down a flight of stairs. I hit a wall and threw out the discs in my back. I couldn't work for over a month—so I lost my job. I couldn't walk, but I could write. Lying on my back for all those weeks, all I could do was write and think. I thought about this idea I'd had for some time but I was so busy at the job I hadn't been able to surface it. During that time I wrote the twenty-five-page business plan for D_parture Spa. I worked the phone and did all sorts of research. Every day I breathed life into the concept.

Be willing to take the long road

It took me two years to convince the airport to let me in. I got a designer who actually designed the store on paper because I knew they would have to see it. I stayed on the phones, making friends with the secretaries, trying to get meetings and feedback. Eventually the airport came to me and said, "We love the idea, but we just gave the space to the Body Shop and we have no more space available for two years." I was disappointed. So I went back to fashion and got a job. Two weeks after I got that job, I got a call that the airport had changed its marketing plan. There would be no Body Shop. They were giving me the space.

Redefine what failure is

Women in business attach failure or success to the bottom line. But there's a period of bootstrapping that occurs when you're growing a business where the concept/model doesn't match your projections. You're not paying yourself, you're messing up your credit, and all your work is not translating into revenues. Women are internalizing that as a failure, but there is no shame in the bootstrapping phase.

Disasters happen; have a plan

After a rock-star start, God rendered me powerless after 9/11. I could not figure my way out of a paper bag. We had just opened in terminal C of Newark Airport in November 2000; then the towers fell and the Transportation Safety Administration changed everything about the airport. Our revenues plummeted. I watched two competitors go out of business. One was a Harvard grad with a strong business background. And there was me. It was frightening. I was broken.

Humbly handle success

Today, I'm more purpose driven. I understand my responsibility with this success. This business is attached to my purpose—to testify that you can achieve whatever you want to achieve. No thing can keep you down.

Connect to the magic of entrepreneurship

You are crafting something out of thin air. Before you put your hands on it, it didn't exist in the world. Sometimes we let reality set into our thinking and ways, but it has no place there.

CHAPTER SIX

Spread the Word: Building Your Brand, Creating Buzz, and Marketing Your Business

Who you are speaks so loudly I can't hear what you're saying.
—*Ralph Waldo Emerson*

Now that you know you've got a market-tested, winning business idea, it's time to get out there and spread the word. Marketing is the lifeblood of any business. You can have the most amazing product or service, but if you don't have a marketing plan, be it word of mouth, Internet, or print advertising, you won't have a successful venture. The problem with marketing is that there is a lot of trial and error. In fact, there's a popular saying in the marketing world attributed to John Wanamaker—"Half the money I spend on advertising is wasted; the trouble is I don't know which half." Furthermore, marketing is more art than science. It's not always based on numbers and logic. The good news is, as black women we have great intuition and can excel at nurturing relationships. These two assets can put you in good stead for marketing success.

Marketing can be as simple as telling friends and family and making a couple of flyers here and there. But if you want to really make your marketing efforts pay off, you have to hustle. There's a popular form of marketing out there for small businesses called guerrilla marketing, which uses time, energy, and imagination as the primary investments. But what I'm talking about is called gangsta marketing—it takes guerrilla marketing to the next level. And though there is no promotion of violence in this strategy, there is a do-or-die quality about getting your name out; a willingness to take risks; a grassroots, in-the-streets approach; and killer results.

But you can't go gangsta without knowing exactly what you are marketing. Who are you as a company? What message are you conveying? Who are you trying to attract? Quite simply, you need a brand. Your brand is not necessarily your logo, although that can be included in your brand. Your brand is who you are and who you are attracting. The brand can be you as a person or your company.

When I first thought about branding *The Mocha Manual,* it was all about the image on the book cover and what she conveyed. She was sassy, upwardly mobile, with a fresh attitude about life and motherhood. That was great! But as the business grew, I became included as part of the brand. In fact, it became a clear business objective to brand myself as the voice of black mommyhood. I was a distinct part of the brand, and as I continue to go around the country speaking about issues for black mothers and writing books for black women, I am continually building the brand of *me,* which is a key part of the Mocha Manual Company.

This brand-building is complex yet important stuff. Send out the wrong message and you'll miss your market completely. To get it right you must first explore and define your company identity and your target market. Take out a pen and paper and answer the following questions:

1. What Is Your Company About? Or What Are You About?

What sets you or your company apart from others who are providing a similar product or service? If you don't know, then you must figure it out before you're in business. What are your core values? What drives you? And as for your company, are you trying to reinvent the wheel or are you creating something that will target a specific audience and attract a certain type of clientele? Are you meeting a specific need? Is your product or service a luxury or an everyday staple? What is the overall intended purpose of your product or service and how does that relate to your anticipated customer base? When you understand fully what your company/brand is about and how it works, then you will be able to market it.

2. Who or What Is Your Market?

Who's your customer? Is she urban chic or a suburban mom? Are you targeting *Fortune* 500 companies or small businesses? Upscale? Mass-market? Affluent or middle-class? What types of words and images would appeal to that customer? The better you identify and understand your customer, the more effective your marketing will be. If you need some help, do a search on the Internet through search engines like Google or Yahoo. Simply type in your product or service to find out who is offering it, how they package it, and how they market it. You can even figure out who their customer base is by simply looking at their pricing, location, and presentation. Some websites may be geared toward high-end clientele, while others target the masses. Try to identify companies that are taking on a similar venture, because those will be your competitors. Along the way you will be able to figure out which products and companies are popular and which aren't. It's always helpful to look at both successful and not-so-successful models so that you can learn the best approaches and mistakes to avoid. Other helpful resources include the U.S. Small Business Administration and its Women's Business Center, which conduct market research on service- and product-based businesses.

What Is Branding?

Once you have clear idea of your company and customer you can start thinking about your brand. Technically, a brand is a label or marker used by a company to identify a product or service distinctively. It is a look and a concept that is identified with the product or services offered by the company. This can include your logo, advertising, website, and packaging. When you think of brand masters like Starbucks, McDonald's, Target, and Louis Vuitton, they all have one thing in common—you know what you're getting and you know who their typical customer is.

In addition to branding your company, several entrepreneurs successfully brand themselves either as part of the company or as the company itself. Many have branded themselves as motivational speakers, experts in their field, or training masters.

Lynette Khalfani Cox began branding herself as "the Money Coach" in 2003, months after regaining her footing after an unexpected layoff. After several years as a successful financial journalist working for Dow Jones (then parent company of the *Wall Street Journal*) and appearing on the air for CNBC and the like, Lynette was a victim of downsizing. "I definitely went through my 'boo-hoo, woe is me' phase. But in short order I was like, Okay, one monkey don't stop the show. I've got to make a move. I always had the seeds of entrepreneurship planted in me and downsizing became the spark for me," she says.

With a good team of advisers, Lynette says she thought long and hard about her handle and thought "the Money Coach" was a good fit because it describes someone who keeps you in shape with your finances. "We did a lot of front-end homework on the concept of my brand," she says. Lynette, a married mother of two in New Jersey, began building her brand with books. In fact, her book was already in progress, but her demanding job didn't give her the time or mental energy to complete it. When she did finish and self-publish her first book, *Zero Debt,* she hired a publicist and worked her old TV connections. A very smart move.

For her first release, Lynette was booked on the Dr. Phil and Jane Pauley shows—the national exposure catapulted her into the big leagues. "The day I appeared on *Dr. Phil,* ten thousand book orders went out the door." *Zero Debt* became a *New York Times* bestseller. Two years later, she wrote *The Money Coach's Guide to Your First Million,* and this time she landed on Oprah's couch talking about it. We don't even have to mention what being on *Oprah* will do for your sales.

"Books are a great calling card to help you attract media attention, establish credibility, and build your brand. I saw the speaking platform and the writing platform as complementary to each other. The brand strategy was about getting on TV and radio talking about the books and getting paid by corporations to conduct money management workshops for their employees," Lynette says. So far, the strategy is working very well. Lynette says her speaking income handily exceeds her book income. And in 2007, she was featured in nearly every personal finance magazine or website, receiving over 300 million media impressions. Now, that's a brand! "Most definitely, my success building my brand as the Money Coach is highlighted by the tremendous amount of media exposure I got," she says.

To begin your winning brand-building campaign, take a cue from Lynette's strategy and do plenty of up-front research and homework.

- Write down some key words to describe your company. For example, *upscale, ethnic, community-oriented, professional, sophisticated, exclusive, family-friendly, classy, fun,* etc.
- Write down some images that are associated with these terms. Yahoo's brand and logo definitely have a connotation of fun, while IBM exudes conservatism and stablity.
- Now think about your customers. What images do they relate to? What would encourage them to buy from you? What names would they connect with? What concepts, such as all-natural or organic, would they relate to?
- Use your friends to test your name and any initial brand messaging ideas. Host an informal focus group or use an e-mail blast. Make sure to ask what they like and dislike, what they would change, and for any suggestions they might have.
- Listen. When you ask for feedback you must take it on board. Don't be so attached to an idea that you're not receptive to constructive criticism.

Branding involves creating the most appropriate image that speaks to all that your company embodies and *could* embody. I say that just to point out that you may not want your logo and name to be too specific, but something that is transformative. Your company may expand toward new ventures but you don't want to be stuck with a logo that confuses customers about what it is you actually offer. Shakara Bridgers, a graduate of UNC Chapel Hill, teamed up with two girlfriends to write and self-publish *The Get 'Em Girl's Guide to Unlocking the Power of Cuisine: A Sassy Girl's Cookbook* and launch www.getemgirls.com. Bridgers and her partners, Joan Davis and Jeniece Isley, brand themselves as "the self-proclaimed princesses of a new urban culinary lifestyle." These three ladies started their success story by doing something based on what they know: being single in the city. And after some informal research in barbershops, workplaces, and churches about what men really want, they realized that the old saying "The way to a man's heart is through his stomach" still held true. So they set out to target the sassy, single professional diva who uses her oven for Tupperware storage (guilty!) with simple recipes to enhance her life and impress her man. As with the Get 'Em Girls, or any other good branding strategy, the style and personality of your company should shine. Your brand distinguishes your company from the others offering similar services and products.

Look Big

Regardless of whether you have a few employees or are a one-man show, you want your brand to look big. Perception is everything. Your brand should project strength and stability—these are the traits associated with big companies—so your clients and customers trust you and your services. If your branding screams "mom and pop," you won't be able to convince your customers of your professionalism, no matter how hard you try.

And don't be afraid to put yourself out there. Robin Wilson, president of Robin Wilson Home, went from executive recruiter to renovation and design manager and learned one valuable branding lesson along the way. "When I first opened, I didn't want to be a showoff and name my company after myself. Instead I called it WSG (Wilson Services Group) Consulting. Huge mistake. No one could remember it. Plus, my expertise and talent are what clients are buying. We rebranded as Robin Wilson Home. Business is booming," Wilson said in an interview in *O* magazine.

Once you've figured out your name, consider your logo and a catchy tagline. You may want to hire a professional to develop your logo or maybe work out a service trade with a graphic designer. Your logo needs to work in a large and small graphic and in color and black and white (what if the gorgeous colors turn to a blotted mess when the logo comes through the fax machine?). Take a cue from the big boys and get a clean, uncomplicated logo in one or two strong colors. Target goes for red. Sprint goes for yellow. And stick with only one or two fonts. This is all part of your corporate identity. If you feel your name and logo are a sheer stroke of genius and should be protected, consider getting a trademark (see box).

PROTECT YOUR BRAND

Now that you've got a fabulous brand, you want to protect it. To do so, you may need a trademark.

What is a trademark? A trademark is any unique word, symbol, name, or device used to identify and distinguish the goods of one seller from the goods of another—think Nike's swoosh, for example. A trademark allows the seller to protect what's trademarked from use and/or misuse by competitors. Trademarks also help prevent confusion or manipulation of consumers, who come to associate distinct attributes—in particular, quality—with a distinct brand.

What can be trademarked? From a branding perspective, the following are assets that can be protected: logos, names, taglines, and packaging. However, these assets can only be trademarked if they meet certain qualifications. A word or phrase that's commonly used or already connected with another product or service in the same industry cannot be trademarked. For example, a generic term like *search engine* can't be trademarked, but a unique name, like Google, can be. However, if your name is generic but used in an industry not typically related to the meaning of the term, you may be able to trademark it. A good example would be Apple computers.

As a general rule, you can trademark your business name if you use it when advertising directly to your customers. If you don't use your business name in direct communication with your customers, you probably can't, because you're not connecting your name to your brand and its attributes. If your business name will be a large part of your marketing, you should consider trademarking it.

You can also trademark your logo and tagline. The first litmus test: Is it unique? What makes a logo unique is the combination of the symbol with the company name, the spatial relationship of the name and symbol, and the logo's colors. If your tagline is a unique phrase, it can also be trademarked. Hallmark's "When you care enough to send the very best" connects a Hallmark brand attribute—quality—to its product. Wal-Mart's tagline, "Save Money. Live Better," shows

(Continued)

you the benefit of their low prices, and Home Depot's "You can do it. We can help"—creates a partnership between you, Home Depot, and your DIY project. It all works.

What's the process and cost? It's not necessarily expensive to trademark something. In the United States, whoever establishes priority in a mark is usually considered the owner of it. In other words, if you're the first company to use a unique mark to identify your products or services, you don't need to register your mark to gain rights to it. You must, however, add the trademark symbol, TM, to the mark you're claiming rights to. But it's still not quite a substitute for registering a mark through the U.S. Patent and Trademark Office (USPTO), which establishes ownership beyond a doubt.

If you file a trademark application with USPTO, it'll ensure no other trademarks similar to yours currently exist. Go to www.uspto.gov to get started. There are two types of registration involved: the right to use and the right to register. The USPTO determines who gets ownership of the mark, which can be complicated if two or more parties are using the same mark. In most cases, the USPTO will grant the first person to use the mark or the first to apply for registration the right to trademark registration. You fill out an application and pay a filing fee.

The whole process can take months. Do your homework, because if your mark closely resembles someone else's, your application will be denied. Keep in mind that the more you differentiate your brand from others in your industry, the easier it'll be to protect. Choose a name and logo that distinctly identify your business and you will protect it from competitors.

Branding Breakthrough Worksheet

1. What's in a name? List three or more possible names for your company:

    a. _____

    b. _____

    c. _____

    Think about this: Is the name easy to say? Easy to spell?

2. List at least three things that describe your company:

    a. _____

    b. _____

    c. _____

3. Do you want to hire a graphic designer instead of creating the image yourself?

    Yes ____   No ____

    Think about this: Are there any goods or services you can offer in exchange for design work?

4. Who is your target customer? Men? Women? Children? Professionals? The elderly?

    _____

    _____

    _____

5. What are they looking for?

_____

_____

_____

6. What is your competitive advantage? (Quicker, easier, ethnicity-specific)

_____

_____

_____

7. Is your service or product:

Affordable ____   High-End ____   Varies ____

8. What other adjectives would you apply to your company? Would a combination of any of these words make a catchy phrase or tagline?

_____

_____

_____

9. Do you see the nature of your company changing in a few years?

Yes ____   No ____

10. What is your company's color scheme?

Bright ____   Dark ____   Neutral ____

11. What is your company's style? Chic? Basic business? Up-scale? Fun? Feminine? Masculine?

_____

_____

_____

12. Are there any metaphors or symbols related to your business industry that come to mind? For example, scales are a common symbol in the legal field, an apple is associated with education, etc.

_____

_____

_____

After you finish this exercise, share your short list with your friends and advisers and get some honest feedback. Try to get feedback from people who are similar to your potential customers—if you're targeting moms, ask moms. If you're targeting young men, get feedback from young men. Whether you are branding yourself or your professional services, doing it well can be a powerful tool for success. It will draw people and opportunities to you like a magnet. Branding is not just about you being better than your competition. It's about getting your prospects to choose you as the _only_ solution to their problem.

With a powerful brand you can:

1. Increase your competitive edge. One of the greatest benefits of having a strong brand is that it creates a sense of individuality and "separateness" in the marketplace so that your clients are able to easily differentiate your company from your competitors. You want to stand out in the crowd, not blend into the pack.

2. Catapult your authentic self into the marketplace. Your brand is deeply rooted in your authentic personal identity. Do you! The goal of personal branding is to be known for who you are as a person and what you stand for—your opinions, values, and beliefs that are visibly expressed by what you say and do, and how you do it. The key here is to keep it real. Brutal honesty has become the must-do marketing move! When you speak the truth, you become a trusted advocate and go-to source. People may not always like the truth, but they will certainly respect you for telling it and always remember that you did.

Remember that when you present a brand, the brand is you. You have to walk it. Live it. Breathe it every day. When I took on the Mocha Manual brand and positioned myself as the spokesperson of pregnancy and motherhood for black women, I had to live and breathe that brand. That means my appearance, speech, and demeanor should be a positive reflection of that brand every day. And while I think I have a great style and an impressive handbag and shoe collection, my one area of weakness is makeup. I just don't like the way I look in makeup. I don't have time for it and I'm not very good at applying it (or so I've told myself for decades). And trust me, I've blown a wad of money trying. But a polished look with an unpolished face is not very fabulous at all! So I had to make sure I was consistent in my brand in all areas of my life. I visited a professional makeup consultant who helped me develop a simple routine that looked natural and very "me." Your everyday appearance and everything from a clean car to fresh breath is a reflection of your brand—you never know where you will meet a prospective client or customer, and this way, you will always be confident enough to pull out your business card and sell yourself.

Personal presentation is even more critical when you are on

the job. "Every time I do a wedding I am doing it for the next client who could be in that room watching my every move and demeanor," says Mayai Chatman, president of Wedding Day Inc. (www.wednday.com), a wedding planning service.

3. Get the biggest bang for your efforts. Your personal brand plan can become your own compass or personal North Star. It can keep you focused and guide all your actions and communications so that you demonstrate authenticity and consistency in all your interactions.

4. Create buzz. You want to be buzzworthy and get noticed. With clear branding you can generate word-of-mouth marketing through the invisible networks that the buzz spreads through. Sharon Sauls is the owner of SKY Neurological Rehabilitation (www.skyneurorehab.com), an outpatient rehab center for people with strokes, traumatic brain injuries, and other neurological disorders serving the Baltimore–Washington, D.C., area. Before Sharon parlayed her health care consulting experience into her own business over ten years ago, she hit the community to create buzz. Sharon and her business partner, Yvette Valiente, hit the streets wearing classy black blazers with a gold SKY logo emblazoned on it. "We wore our blazers and went to as many events as we could afford to to introduce ourselves and the rehab services our company would provide," Sharon says. "People began to connect with our faces, our SKY blazers, and the business, and we were invited to even more industry functions." The blazers were a great (yet professional-looking) tool for generating buzz and getting noticed and remembered by the industry and community.

Solidifying and presenting your brand will connect you with the movers and shakers who will send you referrals, build your credibility, and give you testimonials. It will get people talking about you and stimulate customer-to-customer selling.

5. Establish yourself as an expert and become a celebrity in your area of specialty. Gain name recognition in your area of expertise where it counts the most—in your customer's mind. We'll discuss some ideas for putting yourself out there in the next section.

Marketing Know-How

Like I said, marketing is a lot of trial and error. Many women that I interviewed shared their cautionary tales of money wasted on empty marketing ventures. Marketing is time consuming and requires persistence, research, and money. If you are on a tight budget then you must think beyond the basics, and if you have the means to splurge you want to be sure not to waste your money. The Internet is the great equalizer; it can give you access to millions of customers if you know how to find and attract them. E-mail blasts, newsletters, and websites are amazing tools if harnessed correctly. And most of the women we interviewed placed less emphasis on education and more on tactics like word of mouth and mentorship when discussing what's important for marketing success. Research tells us that personal encounters create a certain level of accountability that written advertisements wouldn't. Your woman's intuition tells you what you know about yourself, that you prefer personal attention. From your man to your bank, you respond to the personal touch. Jinnie English, a licensed clinical social worker and owner of English Consulting, provides therapy and consulting for high-achieving professionals and leaders. When she first launched her business, she went through an array of expensive and ineffective marketing initiatives. After revisiting her strategy she realized that focusing on a niche such as high-powered professionals and offering herself as a specialist with something to teach produced better results. "We became very specific about who we target," English says. As a result, English rebranded her company as Chicago's High Achievers, a relational enhancement firm. Melinda Emerson of Quintessence Multimedia had a similar epiphany: "We became very niche oriented and started doing business in certain industries where we could become specialists. Becoming a specialist sets your company apart and brings in greater revenue," Melinda says.

Sharon Sauls of SKY Rehabilitation says her initial business development/marketing strategy was to find out who was who in the community where she decided to open her first rehabilitation center and meet them (read more about Sharon on pages 269–272). Sharon focused on professionalism and credibility and established relationships with key players in the community and health care professionals who served patients who could be potential clients, such as stroke victims. This method allowed her to be linked to credible sources and well-known patient advocacy groups. Their seal of approval gave her increased publicity. You too can generate more awareness of your company with a few simple, inexpensive strategies:

1. Offer free talks and small-scale seminars. Small seminars are one of the best ways to grow your business and get referrals. Put on your own free talks and seminars, or offer them through your local library or organizations that can put you in front of your ideal clients.

2. Work your website to focus on keywords. Make the most of your website by making sure it gets noticed by people searching for your type of business or service. The key is keywords. If you don't use targeted keywords on your website page names and your website copy, people will never find you through the search engines. Find out which words potential customers are searching for, and sprinkle those words throughout your website copy and your articles too. Go to www.onlinesuccessmap.com for free tools for improving your website's search engine ranking. Consider picking up a book like *Web Marketing for Dummies* or *Search Engine Optimization for Dummies* to make the most of your website. We'll discuss some basic search engine optimization rules in a few minutes.

3. Write articles to demonstrate your expertise. Writing and promoting articles that showcase your expertise can give you lots of free publicity for your business. Write about the latest trends, have an opinion, and take a stand. Publishing articles both online at directories and niche sites as well as offline in print publications will help you stand out and get noticed.

4. Expand your network. You need a large network to grow your business. Develop strategic alliances and ask others to help get the word out for you. Sharon Sauls, our rehabilitation center owner, contacted her local county executive's office, introduced herself, and asked who could introduce her to key health-related decision makers in the county. "In the meantime," she says, "I also scheduled meetings with the health care professionals in the area who frequently see the patients who would need our services to let them know we were bringing a rehabilitation center to the area and their patients." Leverage the power of your connections to promote your business. (We'll discuss networking know-how more later in the chapter.)

5. Create a powerful introduction. What's your thirty-second pitch? Create an introduction that says in as few words as possible who you work with, what their biggest challenge is, and how you help them solve that problem. Don't fall into the trap of trying to run down a laundry list of every product and service you offer. Make it succinct and focus on the benefit you provide. If you sell clothes, say, "We make women look better and feel better!" If you bake cakes, say, "We make special occasions more memorable! Add some pizzazz!" Then get the word out, and ask others to spread it for you too.

6. **Start an e-zine, blog, or podcast.** You need to get in front of your potential customers an average of seven times before they are ready to buy from you. An e-mail newsletter or e-zine is one of the most effective ways to stay in touch with clients and provide value. A blog can be very effective too. It enables you to have a two-way conversation with your audience and develop a voice in your industry.

"We created a weekly newsletter, sent out mass e-mails, and hosted events like 'Girls Bite In,'" says Get 'Em Girls founder and author Shakara Bridgers. "MySpace and YouTube have also been excellent resources."

7. **Get testimonials**. Testimonials from others give your goods or services a stamp of approval. People want to know that others have used your business with success. My friend Christine was bidding for an IT project for a big-name company. She knew she was competing against much larger technology firms. Her proposal for the project included a super-reduced cost in exchange for a testimonial from the marquee company about her work that she could use for future advertising and marketing. The company agreed! She did a great job on the project, but more important, she had a glowing testimonial from a big-name client, which helped her land even more business.

8. **Give stuff away.** It may sound counterintuitive since you're in business to make money, but when you give you get. A friend of mine in London hosted a massage-athon for cancer patients. When he realized there were three radio personalities from the BBC at the event, he offered them free massages. As a result, his

company got free international press coverage. You can also e-mail a coupon to friends or clients offering a free or discounted service or product. If your service is something that people have an interest in, they will forward it on.

9. **Don't forget the old school**. Traditional advertising methods such as print advertising, local newspapers, and radio still work too. Local community centers and church bulletin boards are still great places to post leaflets, flyers, and notices of upcoming events.

Getting Press Coverage

One of the first steps to getting press coverage for yourself or your product is to write a well-crafted press release (see our sample press release on page 273–275). As a fifteen-year veteran of journalism, I can tell you that only the best press releases get read, and releases that come off as amateurish or clueless about what the magazine or editor covers will be quickly discarded. The other secret I will reveal is that journalists and editors are essentially lazy. If we're picking up a press release, we want you to have done all the work for us. And remember, we write stories, not companies, so you have to position your company as a compelling story. That means you need a compelling angle. (Did your product save a life? Is it the next best thing to . . . ?) Let's face it, we like drama! Was there some dramatic event that changed the direction of your life? If your story doesn't have drama, get creative (but honest!). What is special or different about your business? What inspired you to create it?

There's a lot of PR help on the web. Once you draft a release, you have to get it out there. The free Internet-based wire service www.prweb.com lets you put your release out on the "PR wire" for the media to see, and the site has great tips on formatting a press release and some useful templates. I can attest that "checking the wires" is an important part of every journalists' daily or weekly routine. We regularly look there for story ideas so we are not beat to the next hot thing! On that website you also have the option of paying for a higher placement in the PR Web news feeds. Other newswire services are PR Newswire (www.prnewswire .com) and PR Leap (www.prleap.com). Press Blaster (www.press blaster.net) is a great software program to help you distribute your own press releases.

Start with the local media and then approach the national press. Mentioning that you've been featured in other newspapers and magazines adds credibility to your pitch. Read the actual magazine you're pitching. Check out the masthead to see who covers what areas. When I worked for magazines, there was nothing more annoying than receiving a fashion press release with an "I thought you'd be interested in this" note, when I was the editor for personal finance and careers. Know the press cycle. Magazines are typically planning three to six months ahead of time. Don't call a magazine in January or February to pitch your Valentine's Day promotion.

CONNECT TO A CAUSE

Can you attract media attention by attaching your business to a larger cause? There are a number of causes and movements out there, from being environmentally green to health issues to corporate crusades. When you attach yourself to a mission that is larger than you, you get access to more people, you gain credibility, and a greater level of community consciousness is attached to your brand.

Award Yourself

There should be no shame in your game when it comes to going after awards. Nominating yourself for award programs is a great way to generate press. Joining chapters of organizations for women entrepreneurs like the National Association of Women Business Owners (NAWBO) and the National Association of Female Executives (NAFE) is great way to access established annual awards and put yourself in the running.

Contact your local chamber of commerce to see if there are any award programs in your area. Do a Google search of "award programs women entrepreneurs" to turn up a whole list of opportunities.

Get Professional Help

There's a laundry list of do-it-yourself ideas out there. But you may also want to get some professional help. Just make sure you're doing it for the right reasons; there's a lot you can do on your own first. If you do hire an expert consultant, PR firm, or publicist, be prepared to pay from several hundred to thousands of dollars per month. Personal references and word of mouth are often the best ways to get a good PR person. Be sure to get references and interview their clients. Start off with a short contract—say, three months instead of six. This saves you money and gives you time to assess the agency/person during that initial term.

Celebrity Plugs

Getting a celebrity to wear your product, be your client, or use your services is a great promotional tool! Everybody wants to do what celebs are doing. There is now a whole industry out there to get your product included in celebrity gift bags at key award shows. Doreen Motton got her satin slumber collection in the gift bag of the NAACP Image Awards and got a sale and promotional plug from actress Kimberly Elise (*Diary of a Mad Black Woman*) because of it.

If you have a product that may suit a celebrity, use the Internet to locate her publicist or manager and send a sample of your product along with a personal note. Start with local celebrities, including news anchors and local television show hosts. Or if your area has celebrity residents, try wooing them with a special gift basket or gift. Get creative!

If you have a big budget, there are companies that will introduce your product to celebrities at television award shows and the like for a hefty fee. But beware of gimmicks! One company that contacted us charged $1,000 for inclusion in the gift bag, and then you could pay nearly double that for a picture of a celebrity with your product and then a higher price for a picture and testimonial. I gotta tell you, it was shocking what money can buy in terms of endorsements! One of the reputable specialty marketing companies is Backstage Creations (www.backstagecreations.com).

Work the Web

I don't have to sell you on the beauty of the Internet. The Internet can be a small-business owner's dream! The Internet is such a great tool for marketing because you can do a lot of market testing without a great expense. Most of the businesses that run out of money do so by overspending on marketing. You can advertise online for dramatically less than it costs to advertise in the real (or offline) world. And you can communicate instantly with the world with just a few clicks. Two highly successful ways to advertise on the web include keyword advertising on search engines and banner advertising. But remember, the Internet is constantly changing. Some techniques are hot one minute and fizzle out the next, so keep doing your own searches and research to stay on top of current online marketing trends. These will likely always be your least expensive marketing efforts, so it's well worth any time and effort taken to learn new strategies.

Banner Advertising

Banner ads are rectangular ads that usually appear at the top of websites. They can be interactive and have moving/changing elements and a clickable link to your website. There's a lot of debate about the effectiveness of banner ads and whether they've become more of a nuisance than a way to attract consumers. One of the strategies that experts say does work is using niche websites where you know potential customers will be. If there are particular websites that are especially appropriate destinations for your advertising, it's worth contacting such sites to determine what their ad rates and policies are.

Search Engines and Keyword Advertising

Your potential clients search the Internet looking for things just like you do! In fact, according to research by Marketing Sherpa, almost 134 million people in the U.S. regularly use search engines when looking for information online. Of that number, 63 percent look only at the first page of results—at most.

So if you want your site to be there, there is a strategy called search marketing—a catchall term for search engine optimization and pay-per-click advertising—that you can put to work for your business.

Search engine optimization covers all the different ways to organically move your website up in the rankings of the free search engines. These are called "natural" listings. You can improve your ranking by giving the search engines what they're looking for. This should be the core of your Internet marketing strategy. Here are some of the most popular SEO strategies:

1. **Find the hottest keywords for your market.** This is the starting point for any search marketing campaign. If you are a technology consulting firm, then you have to spend some time playing with keyword searches to figure out what words people use when they search for a technology consulting firm. Potential keywords would include "technology solutions" and "database programming." Play around with different possibilities. Think like your customer to figure out what search terms they may use to find a company with your services.

2. **Plug keywords into the right locations in your copy and website code.** Your website is full of hot spots that search engine "spiders" check regularly looking for keywords. Put your keywords in the headlines, subheads, and body copy of your web pages. In the HTML or other code behind your site, place keywords in anchor text, alt text, title tags, image tags, and meta tags. But don't overload them. Those spiders are getting smart—when they see too many keywords they detect fraud and keep it moving. Make sure the keywords are used frequently but naturally.

3. **Use keywords that relate directly to your content.** If you sprinkle keywords like "guaranteed weight loss" through a site that sells shoes, search engines will ignore you. Your keywords will work best if they reflect what your site is about.

4. **Update content regularly.** The more fresh, relevant content they find, the higher the search engine spiders are likely to

rank your site. Keep all the copy on your pages current, including any changes or updates to your business or products. And archive your newsletters or bulletins on your site. A blog or forum also keeps people heading back for regular updates and discussion.

5. Make it natural. Make sure you integrate your keywords as naturally as possible into your copy. You won't keep your visitors' attention if the text on your site is just a jumbled bunch of keywords.

6. Get links from other websites that are considered reputable and relevant. Natural and relevant links are search engine gold. Focus your strategy on requesting one-way links from sites with high natural rankings in search engines. Distributing free articles and press releases is a great way to get quality inbound links.

7. Be a social butterfly. Don't forget the power of social networking online. By taking part in online communities or uploading videos to a site like YouTube, you can drive new traffic to your website and get new sites linking to yours.

KEYWORDS/PAY-PER-CLICK ADVERTISING

When you do a search you'll probably notice a bunch of "sponsored links" or similarly named ads to the right of or above your results listings. These links show up because of the words you typed into your search query. You pay for keywords related to your site, and when people search your specific keywords, your ad comes up. The good news is you only pay when someone clicks through to your site. And with some programs you can control how much you want to spend each month. Google's program, for example, is called AdWords (www.adwords.google

.com). Yahoo's program can be found at sem.smallbusiness .yahoo.com. When you use AdWords your ad can be shown on Earthlink, AOL, and Ask in addition to Google. Because they are tied to keywords, you are more likely to get customers who actually want your product or service. More good news about pay-per-click ads:

Instant gratification. PPC ads show up immediately. You can drive traffic to your site right away, even if you haven't been tapped by search engines yet.

You only pay for results. No matter how many times your ad is displayed, you pay only when someone clicks on it. And by watching your results carefully, you can determine how well each ad is converting and if it's worth continuing.

It's a great testing tool. With PPC, you can run several ads simultaneously, allowing you to see very quickly which ones work best. Test your keywords this way and use the best ones on your site to boost your organic search results.

You can dramatically improve your search engine rankings and direct quality, targeted traffic to your website—often while sitting in your pj's and without spending a single dime. Ain't marketing grand!

Work the Room

For some businesses, no matter how worldwide the web is, nothing beats one-on-one contact. In fact, no marketing strategy is complete without some elements of both. Of course, you can't spend all your time networking when you need to be running your business. Smart networkers know that being out there is one thing, but converting those contacts into meaningful relationships is really where you strike gold.

Networking is not about shaking hands and handing out business cards. It's about building relationships—building "social capital," as some business gurus like to call it. To become a networking diva, you have to master certain skills and traits.

Follow through. This is overwhelmingly the most common quality of successful networkers. They follow up with an e-mail or phone call.

Use technology. Invest in a customer/contact relationship manager (CRM) system, which automates your contact with customers and colleagues. Storing your contacts in an e-mail system like Outlook is not enough.

Have a positive attitude. Leave your "angry black female" suit at home. People respond to warmth, friendliness, sincerity, and a positive attitude. Nobody likes a sourpuss.

Be a good listener. It is not all about you. A successful networker is not just waiting for her chance to pitch; you have to listen. When you really listen well you can hear opportunities and partnerships in the conversation. If you're rehearsing in your head what you want to say, you will hear and learn nothing.

Help others. Again, think beyond yourself. Sometimes you can connect other people just for the sake of helping others out even when there is no immediate benefit to you.

Do the WORK to network. It's not net-sit or net-eat, honey; it's called net-working for a reason. To work your network, manage your contacts with contact management software, organize your e-mail address files, and carry any referral partners' business cards as well as your own. Set up appointments to get better acquainted with new contacts so you can learn as much about them as possible and truly become part of each other's networks.

When you put in the appropriate amount of time to work and build your social capital, you will have business referred to you over and over again. You will have other people doing your job—talking about your company and boosting your brand awareness. Then, my dear, you are a marketing maven!

The Mocha Mix
My Most Creative Marketing Strategy

* * * * * * * * * * * * * * * * * * *

I have to be creative because I am very budget conscious. We go to events, place products in other businesses and restaurant bathrooms, send samples to dance studios, host raffles for schools, and seek out sponsorship and community-based collaborations. These strategies have been very useful.
— TRICIALEE RILEY, owner of Polish Bar of Brooklyn, New York (www.polishbarbrooklyn.com)

I've done everything and have wasted a lot of money. Now I do more networking and really use my professional relationships and things that are low cost, like e-mail. Our company offers psychotherapy specially tailored for high-achieving professionals. So we try to educate people on what therapy is because everyone is not ready for it. We want people who value it. When we market, we are very specific about who we target.
— JINNIE ENGLISH, president of Chicago's High Achievers, Illinois (www.chicagoshighachievers.com)

Networking is most important, but you have to be prepared and do your research first.
— MARSHA BURNETT, president of Musical Directions, New York/Detroit/Los Angeles/London (www.musical directions.com)

My initial business development/marketing strategy was to meet the "who's who" in the community where we decided to open our first rehabilitation center.
— SHARON SAULS, CEO of SKY Neurological Rehabilitation, Maryland (www.skyneurorehab.com)

Word of mouth is my primary marketing tool. That brings in about 75 percent of our business. The other 10 percent comes from the website, and about 5 percent from networking with celebs and other makeup artists.
— ANDREA FAIRWEATHER, CEO of Fairweather Faces, New York/Los Angeles (www.fairweatherfaces.com)

One of the most important things you can have for good marketing is cash. Set aside funds for promotion and marketing of the business every month. You must understand the value of promotion and be willing to invest the money to do it properly.
— KAREN TAYLOR BASS, president and CEO of Taylor Made Media, New York (www.taylormademediapr.com)

To launch my photography business, I looked for local charities and other worthy organizations that were having auctions (live/silent) as part of their fund-raising efforts. I donated a set of photographs, the cost of which was easily offset by any additional prints or other photographic services ordered by the winner. Plus, my name and company was yelled out in front of a large crowd of people!
— SARA HUNTER, photographer, Fairburn, Georgia

INN STYLE

Monique Greenwood, owner of four Akwaaba bed-and-breakfasts, and co-owner with her husband of Akwaaba Properties Inc., a real estate development company in Bedford-Stuyvesant, Brooklyn, whose holdings also include a retail strip that houses an upscale coffeehouse, bookstore, antique shop, restaurant, and hair salon

Monique Greenwood wrote the book on how to turn your dreams into reality. Literally. The onetime editor in chief of Essence *is the author of* Having What Matters: The Black Woman's Guide to Creating the Life You Really Want. *In the book, the sassy, effervescent Greenwood speaks to black women about having fulfilling work, loving relationships, and a sense of purpose. But before she wrote the book, she lived the life of a mother, wife, innkeeper, entrepreneur, and multitasking master.*

Now she adds minimogul to her long list of accomplishments. Greenwood owns four luxury bed-and-breakfast inns, the world-famous Akwaaba Mansion (Brooklyn, New York), Akwaaba D.C. (Washington, D.C.), Akwaaba by the Sea (Cape May, New Jersey), and Akwaaba in the Bayou (New Orleans, Louisiana).

For much of Monique's early days she wanted to be a fashion editor. She grew up as one of five children and attended Howard University, becoming the first person to graduate college in the history of her family. She landed at Fairchild Publications via a minority training program for young journalists and later became lifestyle editor, associate publisher, and eventually editor in chief of a children's fashion magazine; then she left Fairchild Publications to join Essence.

Monique built her growing bed-and-breakfast empire by focusing on what she's good at and working around her weaknesses—one of her critical tips for success. "Cooking is just not my thing. I can only make five breakfasts. If someone stays six nights, I ask them, 'What was your favorite?'" she says.

Greenwood shares her other advice for business building:

Be willing to wait for it

For years I kept driving by the mansion in Brooklyn. It was abandoned. Kids saw it as a haunted house. I did some research and found out it had been vacated by the Lilly family. Every day or every week I would drive by the house. I would leave notes under the door: "If you're looking to sell, please call me . . ." I came by at 9:00 A.M. most every morning. One day I saw someone outside working in the yard. I approached him. He was actually related to the owners. There was a lot of interest in the house, but I was able to get in touch with the family and tell them about my plans. I wasn't an investor; I wanted to live there. It was a very stressful ordeal. The family backed out several times. We were in contract for three years. When we finally got into the house, there was no plumbing and no electrical. Nine months after moving in, we opened up.

Become a student of your trade

I spent a lot of time staying at inns and keeping a journal of what I liked and disliked. I remember an inn that used music as a sign that breakfast was ready. I liked that. Or the inn that left room journals for guests to write about their stay for others to read. I took aspiring innkeepers' workshops and read lots of books.

Start with a side hustle

Dip your feet in the water a little bit at first. Can you start small or apprentice to someone else? Then ask yourself, Do I have the aptitude, patience, and passion for this?

In the early days, my husband and I were still working at our jobs. So we could only accept guests on the weekends and on days when one of us could take off or work from home. We were basically qualifying calls first, before accepting reservations. To everyone else we would say that we were booked. Unknowingly, we created this demand and buzz because we were always "booked."

Keep it in the family

My daughter was three years old when we opened the first inn. I thought, What a great life, the world comes to her breakfast table every morning. We taught her how to wake quietly and be tidy.

Focus on what you love, Delegate, and know when to step out of the process

I'm still making breakfast every day. I took myself out of housekeeping and reservations a few years ago, but I am still very much the innkeeper.

Find the perfect match for your passions

I'm really into design; I would watch HGTV religiously. I love architecture. I'm a closet interior decorator, and I enjoy entertaining, good presentation, and meeting new people, so my business is a perfect fit for me.

Do your research

Do your homework. Make sure you believe it can work. Get everything you can from your current job and bone up on any ancillary skills. Can you make your former employer a client? Don't leave leaning on your new business to fully support you in the beginning.

Take action

After I took the innkeeping course and realized I could make real money at this, I left my job at *Essence* within six months. But in my gut I knew I was leaving way before then. You often know before you are willing to act.

Get past the down times and find your inner voice

There were many days when I was lying in the bed looking at the ceiling wondering why I chose this. But you have to stop and listen to your own voice. Remember why you're doing what you're doing. If you don't stop to listen to your own voice, the only audible voice will be that of the naysayers.

Revisit plans

I first envisioned the Brooklyn Akwaaba as a place for local residents to put up visiting relatives. I saw it as an asset to the community. I thought everyone would embrace the inn, but they did not. At first I was deflated that the neighbors didn't see my vision. But I had to let that be their issue and I had to stay focused.

Be the queen of plan Bs

I always have four plan Bs. Then you can have confidence that you will succeed. If you have everything riding on one thing, you're setting yourself up for failure. When I go into a plan, my backup plans are built into the plan—flip it into this, turn it into that—so that I can't fail. I don't accept failures.

Visualize the life you want

My goal was to retire at fifty and have a house in four cities, one for every season. For me, that's what it's all about.

Live with no regrets

Entrepreneurs are the new American idols. Everyone wants to be the editor in chief of their life.

CHAPTER SEVEN

Crank It Up! How to Take Your Business to the Next Level

Always bear in mind that your own resolution to succeed
is more important than any other one thing.

—*Abraham Lincoln*

Up until this point, you've been probably operating your business in side-hustle mode. That's good. It's best to get the all the groundwork of business-building under way while you still have a steady paycheck to fall back on. But you probably didn't buy this book for tips on staying in side-hustle mode. So now that you've got your passion-focused business, built up a strong team, maintained good financial procedures, and know how to market yourself, it's time to focus on growth.

Just like a real baby, your business baby has a life cycle of its own. A business should go from start-up to initial growth, maturation, and then positioning for payout or an exit plan. Yes, at some point, your business baby may fly without you. To have a real business—one that reaps real financial rewards—you have to build your company, keep it growing, and then, years later, make it attractive for sale. I love running the Mocha Manual Company, but I have warm and fuzzy dreams about the day my maternity- and infant-wear line is purchased by a major apparel company! Of course, that would involve a lucrative deal that allows me to sit back and still get paid for my years of hard work while I do nothing (my ultimate fantasy!), focus on nonprofit work, or start another business.

But for now, our goal is to get you from small fry to Big Mac and turn your side hustle into your main event. To do so, you need to put certain strategies and systems into place. Some of these are just ramped-up versions of principles we've already discussed, like marketing your business and staying focused on your niche, but you can also explore new strategies such as product/service diversification, thinking internationally, and applying for minority business certification to open up a whole new world of clients, customers, and profits. You will also need a revised business plan that reflects the next phase for your company. Making use of all of these moves will help ensure that your business remains viable and insulated from market trends and seasonal swings, so that you can continue to boost your revenues and protect your profits.

In this chapter we'll consider a range of growth strategies, from forging joint ventures with key players to how putting yourself in play for large government contracts. First we start with your mind. Let's get your thinking aligned with growing your business. To do so, you have to think like a CEO.

Ten Growth Strategies to Get Your Side Hustle to the Next Level

1. FOCUS ON A NICHE

We've discussed the power of the niche in the start-up phase in earlier chapters, but as you move into the growth phase, you want to make sure your focus is on growing within your niche instead of expanding outside of it. I know it is hard to resist, ladies, but you simply cannot be all things to all people. As women, we should know this well. We tried the "I can bring home the bacon, fry it up in a pan, and never ever let you forget you're a man" thing, but now we're exhausted. In our infinite wisdom we realized we needed to focus on what we do best. Many entrepreneurs have exhausted themselves and all of their resources trying to be all things to all people. The ability to offer a gazillion products under one roof is great for Wal-Mart but not so great for most small enterprises. If you want to get rich, focus on a niche, become an expert in that field, and service that niche like nobody else.

2. Build a Professional Advisory Committee

We've talked about building a team and surrounding yourself with the right people. For many entrepreneurs, this process often happens informally. To get to the next level, you need a more formal advisory board of business professionals with expertise in all areas of your business. Your board should include members with expertise related to your short-term goals and others who can help with more long-term planning. Attend industry conferences to find seasoned professionals. Open up the yellow pages and call competitors from different regions or neighborhoods. Then research their staff to see if there are any possible matches. Look into the SBA's SCORE (Service Corps of Retired Executives) program, a national mentoring service for entrepreneurs.

If you have attracted a top adviser who asks for equity in your company, make sure you structure the compensation over time such as annually or quarterly, instead of making an up-front payment. If you aren't ready to give away equity, consider a small cash payment to your advisers for conference calls or board meetings, or covering certain expenses instead.

3. DIVERSIFY

I don't have to tell you about all the clichéd expressions about the folly of being undiversified in life and love. Don't put your eggs in one basket, don't be a one-trick pony—they're all based on the concept that you should spread yourself around among options, backup plans, and strategies.

No matter how hot your product or how large your marquee client, if you solely rely on one product, one type of service, or one client, you are putting your company at great risk. This is different from focusing on a niche. At the Mocha Manual Company, our niche is black women who are mothers or moms-to-be. In that niche our products are diversified in that we provide for the expectant mom, the new mom, and her baby. Our future product offerings will support black mothers in other areas of their life, from careers to finances, but our niche among black mothers remains the same. In the business world, there is no greater cautionary tale about the dangers of being a one-trick pony than the fallout from 9/11 and the dot-com bust. Companies that were solely involved with the travel industry or solely relied on dot-coms as clients took a severe drubbing when things took an unexpected turn for the worse.

When you are diversified you are protected from being over-reliant on specific clients or a single product. Let me tell you a stock market secret that was a real *aha!* moment for me. Here's an important lesson I picked up covering Wall Street for over a decade: People invest or don't invest in the stock market because they believe that the stock market has to go up for you to make money. But the truth is, when stocks go up people make money, and when stocks tank other people make money. I assure you that even when the market tanks three hundred points in one day, somewhere there is a large group of people doing a happy dance. I've seen them. One person's pain is another's pleasure. The trick to investing wisely is putting yourself on both sides of the equation. If you only ride one side, you may be in for some bumps and bruises.

It's the same with your business. By diversifying, you can smooth out the seasonal peaks and valleys that can occur in many types of businesses. And you provide a way to grow. A company that cannot grow in product and service options cannot get to the next level. Diversification means adding clients, customers, products, and services. And every savvy businesswoman needs this.

4. Generate Repeat Business

Remember this rule: having a big-name client is great, but having repeat customers is even better. Your company needs repeat business to grow. When you take on too much business from any one client you always risk not cultivating new clients properly or being innovative with new products and offerings. I heard this a lot from the women who were publicists, ran consulting firms, or had IT-related firms who answered our survey. Remember the one-hit-wonder singer Oran "Juice" Jones? Imagine if you were the publicist for Oran "Juice" Jones. When you heard "I saw you and him walking in the rain . . ." on the radio all day every day, and everybody on the street was quoting his "alley-cat-coat-wearing, Hush Puppy–shoe-wearing" dis-and-dismiss monologue, you probably thought this man's success would never end.

You may have foolishly solely focused on him, even letting other clients go to give Juice your full attention. But from a long-term perspective, it would have been better to use the big earnings from Juice to hire staffers to help keep your other clients on board. Or you could have broadened your business scope to go from publicist to manager, thereby giving you a role that wouldn't necessarily end when the newspapers and magazines lost interest.

On the other hand, what if you own a travel company or service provider that focuses only on the airline industry? I met a supersmart business owner named Vanessa at a Mocha Manual event in Atlanta. At one point, Vanessa was earning over $100,000 a year providing promotional T-shirts and other items to large airline companies. She had some of the largest carriers, like Delta Air Lines, as her longtime clients. Then came 9/11. Now, remember my "one person's pain is another's pleasure" analogy. When the airlines hit a wall, you couldn't find a rental car anywhere in the country, let alone one at an affordable price. The airlines' pain was the car rental companies' pure pleasure as more people drove to their destinations. If Vanessa had maintained her niche servicing the travel industry but was diversified within that niche by having clients in different areas of travel, from rental car to cruise companies, she would have been better buffered from the downturn. Her business took a severe hit. At one point she contemplated giving up. Lucky for Vanessa, she was able to able to get new clients. Of course, by this point, everyone else was clamoring to do the same, so the battle was even harder. But within a year she had recovered nicely. She learned a lesson she'll never forget.

Many businesses didn't fare as well. Don't get caught out there! Apply the pleasure/pain principle to your business.

Tough Times Tip: A savvy business owner should always think one step ahead. That includes contingency planning for market changes. Be aware of who would benefit from a downturn in your industry and think of ways to position your business to service them.

As a general rule of thumb the amount of business you get from one client should not exceed 30 percent of your revenues. If you have a client who contributes more than that, it's time to craft a diversification plan.

How can you expand your product or service offerings? If you're a caterer, can you also offer party and event planning services? If you offer a service, how could your pricing be affected by an economic downturn? How would you respond? For example, let's say you own a spa. People go to the spa with their discretionary income—their "play" money. If times got tough and "play" money turned into mortgage and rent money, how would your business adapt? Well, you could go upmarket. The über-rich aren't concerned much about economic downturns. They've learned the secret of stashing away for a rainy day, so you could market exclusively to them.

Or you could launch your own product line (or sell a variety of already existing hot products) so that when people go into DIY mode, they can still have spa-like results at home with your products. If you're going for the rich and famous, what services do you have in place now to court them? Perhaps a private client day, where the spa is closed to the general public and only your moneybags clients are seen. The superwealthy love exclusivity! If a product line sounds more your speed, start asking your clients what part of the spa experience they wish they could duplicate at home. What types of products are your top sellers? Introduce your clients to great products that aren't easily available in your area so people will have to come to you to get them. A little diversification planning can go a long way.

Here are some other factors to consider in the growth phase:

- Is your core business sufficiently established to undertake developing new clients, services, or products?
- Do you have the money to execute the plan? If not, how can you get it?
- Have you figured out how long you will pursue your diversification strategy before you determine whether it's working?
- What is your plan B? Plan C?
- What trends or possible events support your diversification plans? Do the research.
- Is it possible to acquire a different but complementary type of company?
- Can you start another company/subsidiary or consider a joint venture?

Start small by making it a goal to add one to three new clients in one year or less. If you offer a product, look for one to three additional customer bases or begin plans to develop a new product. Remember, successful diversification always leads to growth.

5. STOMP WITH THE BIG BOYS

You didn't get into business to play small! You want to roll with the big boys! The only way to roll with the big boys is to actually align yourself with a larger company and benefit from their mass. We've looked at this concept on a smaller scale in terms of marketing your business and reaching a wider audience. As you grow your business, you want to keep looking for the bigger company or organization to partner with. It may be an established business, a trade association, or even a well-funded nonprofit. They've spent years building a solid customer base and you need to tap into their customers instead of trying to reinvent the wheel yourself. In the marketing world, this is called forming "host-beneficiary" relationships—and it is the single most effective way to quickly attract a critical mass of qualified customers to a new business. Instead of beating the streets for new customers, you can access someone else's established group of consumers and kick-start your sales.

The idea is that you promote yourself to their database of customers with a special offer presented as a gift from the larger business. This arrangement is a sweet deal because you as the start-up or beneficiary can instantly reach large numbers of prospects using an already established, well-respected vehicle—the host. The host participates because it's a way to reward loyal customers without incurring any costs. The rookie gets new customers, and the veteran looks good, as you'll see below.

Valerie Morris used this strategy when she opened her boutique in the D.C. metro area. She knew her target market was professional women who drove certain types of cars and patronized certain types of salons. She approached the local BMW dealer about giving a coupon for a free $100 wrap dress to every woman on their customer mailing list as a thank-you for their BMW patronage. The recipients would have to bring the coupon to the boutique to claim the prize. This was a great customer loyalty giveaway for BMW and it got key women (women with money) into the boutique. Over five hundred women responded and spent, on average, $300 on additional merchandise when they were in the store. That was just on their first visit! I should mention that the dress cost her about $18 wholesale. So she spent $9,000 (five hundred women at $18 per giveaway dress) and made $150,000 in sales (five hundred women times $300 average per sale), and she had the potential to earn more from those customers. Valerie was strategically building her clientele.

This is called working smart. Don't try to do all the work. Piggyback on someone else who's already done it for you! To make sure you get it right:

- **Make sure you've precisely defined your target audience.** Get focused! "Women age thirty-five to forty-seven" isn't enough. Create a detailed profile of your target customer, including what they drive, where they shop, and how they spend their free time.
- **Identify your "big dog."** Find local and national businesses and organizations that serve the same market segments. That will help ensure you get the right initial customers and repeat business. Plus allying with well-known names gives you instant credibility.
- **Have a clear offer.** Develop a free or deeply discounted product or service that has a high perceived value for the customer with a low dollar cost for you. Tanya Coleman runs a computer support business in Greensboro, North Carolina. She offered a voucher worth two free hours of computer repair to the small-business clients of an established local accountant. After a successful response she used that accountancy as a referral to approach a statewide

trade association for accountants (the first accounting firm was a member) and offered a similar deal to all of its members.

- **Pitch properly.** When you pitch the plan, highlight the benefits to the host business. Emphasize that it's a virtually free and effortless way to reward their customers/members.

- **Do the work for them.** Create a draft "offer" letter for the host to use on their own letterhead that can be easily sent to the host's customers. This will help put the plan into motion quickly and show how easy it will be for them to participate. Some businesses may allow your letter to be inserted in their monthly invoices or newsletters at no cost. Others may ask that you pay for an additional mailing. If so, it's still a small price to pay for accessing their database.

- **Make the conversion.** Have a strategy to convert redeemers to repeat customers—the actual point of all this. Whether you're trying to lure customers into your boutique to try more merchandise or your online store to do the same, be clear about how you plan to keep the customers you attract.

- **Keep looking for bigger partners.** To give your business sustainability, keep seeking to align yourself with established businesses. Start with a large local business and keep moving up in size until you can't go any further.

6. Position Yourself to Receive Corporate Funding

Every year corporations spend millions of dollars on cause-related marketing and event sponsorships. Market yourself as a desirable partner to an established business that is seeking the kinds of customers you already have. Larger businesses are looking to attract new customers too—from soccer moms to black female professionals to people who invest—so there's a complementary company out there that wants access to the customers you already have. You may have an event you want to host. Instead of footing all of the expense yourself, think of who else may be interested in the consumers you can attract. Attract sponsors with a well-written sponsorship proposal that shows you are offering a solid marketing investment to the sponsor. To make sure you're well positioned to attract sponsors:

- **Create a list of companies that are headquartered or have sizable regional offices in your area.**
- **Look at your competition.** Are they getting sponsors? If so, from which companies? Can you approach those same companies or their competitors?
- **Think about your organization's reach.** Do you have an established marketing effort in place so that you can keep in touch with your clients through e-mail, a website, events, newsletters, conferences, television, radio, or print advertising? The more avenues you have that can include the potential sponsor's logo or information, the stronger you proposal will be.
- **Consider your organization's demographics.** Is there recent information about who participates and why? Where they live or their income levels? Whether they are repeat users? Whether they are young families, empty-nesters, stay-at-home moms, or teens? Your job is to know your customer well and then find a sponsor that wants that customer. Then you will need the data to show the potential

sponsor that you have exactly the kind of customer he wants.

- **Target your sponsors.** Do you have testimonials from a corporate executive about the value of your organization to its community of users? Do you feature those in press kits or other marketing materials?

> **Tough Times Tip:** If your business can survive with just a few key clients, consider offering those clients a discount in a down market. It's worth it to give big clients a price break rather than lose them.

7. SEEK FINANCING

Consider taking on partners/investors/financing that can help you grow. Yes, it's your baby. And yes, you've put a lot of blood, sweat, and tears into your business. But eventually you may need help. At some point, if you really want to take your business to the next level you may need more capital than you currently have to get you there. Or you may need to buy access to key players and relationships that you may not have.

Either way, don't get caught in the "bootstrap trap." Sure, cobbling together money from credit cards, 401(k), IRA, savings, home equity, or friends and relatives is how most entrepreneurs (particularly those interviewed for this book) started their business, but that doesn't mean it is the only option available to you. Whether you choose a bank, various agencies, a venture capitalist, an angel investor, or a private investor, do your research first to determine what kind of financing is best for your company.

A lot of women, especially black women, are risk averse when it comes to loans and borrowing other people's money. We don't want to owe nobody nothing! And while we are clearly risk takers if we embark on the path of entrepreneurship, we can be very conservative with our financing needs. Through the course of researching this book, I met several women who were successfully running moneymaking businesses but suddenly became afraid of failure when it came to borrowing money. If you have a track record of solid sales, why would that change now if you have even more money to market your business or bring in needed expertise? This is not the time to get fearful. Yes, it's a big responsibility. But you can handle it by sticking to your business plan and implementing the strategies needed to succeed.

If you're looking for a small business loan, the SBA's Office of Women's Business Ownership is a good place to start (www.sba .gov/onlinewbc/wbc.pdf). Their Women's Business Centers program is a national network of more than a hundred resource centers that have been established to assist women in start-up and growing companies.

There are additional opportunities for financing for black women through the SBA. The Department of Commerce's Minority Business Development Agency funds Business Development Centers around the country that work with minority-owned entrepreneurs. There's also the National Bankers Association in Washington, D.C., which represents minority-owned banks that loan to minority-owned businesses. Check out the appendix for more loan programs that black women can take advantage of.

Be sure to read all the fine print, terms, and conditions of any financing, whether it's a loan or otherwise. Also, don't assume that just because it's a government program for small business owners or black women that it's the best loan for you. Some may require that you use your home as collateral or the interest rate may not be so great.

8. Get Minority-Owned Business Certification to Put Your Company in Play to Win Large Government and Corporate Contracts

Depending on the nature of your business, tapping into large municipal, corporate, and government contracts can be big business. Cities, states, corporations, and the federal government need products and services for their employees and constituents too. From construction firms to training to catering to event management, these entities need these services and often have large budgets allocated for using minority-owned businesses. Becoming certified as a woman-owned business (WBE), minority-owned business (MBE), or disadvantaged business enterprise (DBE) and selling to local, state, and federal government entities and large corporations is the first step in growing to the next level.

Fortune 500 companies are required by the federal government and their own corporate guidelines to use diverse suppliers for their needs. Having your minority certification makes you a more desirable vendor or service provider to big businesses too.

You can quickly grow big and reach the million-dollar milestone by selling products and services to deep-pocketed entities. Contracting budgets for government agencies and large corporations are huge. Most major municipalities (cities, counties, parishes) in major metropolitan areas have specific goals for contracting with DBE, MBE, and WBE firms. For example, the city of Dallas lists the following minority supplier goals for city-funded contracts:

- Construction: 25.00 percent
- Architectural and Engineering: 25.66 percent
- Other Professional: 36.30 percent

- Other Services: 23.80 percent
- Goods: 18.00 percent

In this example, if the annual city budget is $100 million for architectural and engineering services, which is typical, over $25 million will be subcontracted to DBE-certified architectural and engineering firms. If you get even a small piece of that pie you can score big!

Karen Taylor Bass knows the benefits of receiving minority business status. Her company was recently certified, and through the mentoring she received during the process, she met hundreds of black women landing million-dollar contracts and up for their goods and services. "For months that application just sat there. It was twenty-plus pages and I just didn't set aside the time. When my friend got that million-dollar contract, I stopped immediately and filled it out. I was like, Girl, I can't afford not to get this done."

The beauty of a government contract, in addition to the larger amounts, is that they are generally longer term (such as a one-year contract for landscaping services or a two-year contract for promotional products). A more lucrative, longer-term contract will enable you to hire employees and grow your business with the peace of mind that you have a commitment (in the form of a contract) from a relatively stable entity. Different clients sometimes require certifications from different certification agencies. Though the certification process can vary from one agency to another, it is generally a straightforward, painless process involving paperwork, documentation, and reasonable application fees. It is well worth the effort.

To simplify the process, consider three general levels of certification: local, state, and federal government or private corporations. Each of these levels requires a specific certification and uses different nomenclature (and acronyms) to describe the certification.

What do the acronyms mean?

ACRONYM*	NAME OF CERTIFICATION	ENTITIES THAT TYPICALLY USES THIS ACRONYM
WBE	Woman-owned Business Enterprise	Private corporations and federal government
MBE	Minority-owned Business Enterprise	Local government or quasi-government entities (e.g., cities, counties, transit agencies, airports)
DBE	Disadvantaged Business Enterprise	Local and state agencies
WOSB	Woman-owned Small Business	Federal government
SDB	Small Disadvantaged Business	Federal government
HUB	Historically Underutilized Business	State or federal government

*The acronyms vary between regions and entities. Check with your local certification agency to determine specific certification descriptions.

Certification Process

The process for certification may seem more complicated than it actually is. If you have the ambition and organizational skills to start your own business, you can certainly tackle the certification process. Once you determine the type of certification that you need (depending on the type of agency that you would like to have as a client), the process typically involves completing an application, providing documentation, and paying an application fee of $300 or more. View it as a critical investment in your business. Look in the yellow pages and find a local SBA or Small Business Development Corp. office for advice. Also, any small business organization for women, such as the National Association of Women Business Owners or the Association of Black Women-Owned Enterprises, can provide coaching and assistance.

You can also contact the Women's Business Enterprise National Council (WBENC) at 202-872-5515. WBENC is the nation's leading third-party certifier of WBEs. It serves as a one-stop shop for certification, meaning that when you get WBENC certified, the certification is accepted by thousands of major corporations, along with most government and federal agencies. It is a widely accepted umbrella certification and having it is usually much quicker than dealing with state or federal agencies directly. WBENC certification can be granted within sixty to ninety days of submission of all your paperwork.

In general, the following information may be required for certification:

- Business history, board, and key management
- Legal structure, including articles of incorporation or assumed-name certification

- Evidence of gender and/or minority status of owner(s)
- Financial statements and tax returns
- List of all employees (if any) and itemized payroll

The process also usually includes a personal visit to your office from a representative of the certification agency. The purpose of the visit is to verify that you are indeed in responsible charge of the business.

Each certifying agency has its own process for certification. In addition, different states and regions within the state have unique requirements. This is where it gets tricky. To simplify the process, many states have implemented a "unified certification" policy. In this case, regional agencies and the state will recognize certifications from other regions, reducing the amount of paperwork required to become certified with numerous regional agencies. Consult your certification agency for details about the requirements specific to that agency.

9. Go global

It's a big world out there. And there's plenty of money to be made beyond our shores. To grow your company, you may want tap into a new pool of customers elsewhere. If possible start with Canada or the UK, where there aren't any language barrier concerns. Going global is much easier these days if you sell a product. The web has become the great equalizer and some e-commerce solutions will convert the currency for you at checkout. Done! To be honest, when I launched our United Kingdom website I did not follow any of the steps I'm about to recommend. Since I used to work and live in London, I've always felt I have one foot in each country. Having worked as a journalist in London, I have an extensive network of press contacts and an amazing friend, Richard Adeshiyan, who is the PR guru for black folks in London. When I was invited to host a seminar and have a booth at one of England's biggest expo-type events for black women, I figured I better have a website too. Richard already had radio and newspaper interviews lined up, so I knew I could get publicity for the site. I quickly cobbled together a UK front page, changing the intro language to suit UK black women (changing *mom* to *mum*; using *Afro-Caribbean* instead of *African-American*), and voilà! The Mocha Manual went international. I was on BBC Radio, was featured in the *Guardian* newspaper, and snagged articles in the two largest black national newspapers. But here's a smarter way to go about it:

1. **Prepare an international business plan to evaluate your needs and set your goals.** It's essential to assess your readiness and commitment to grow internationally before you get started. It does not have to be extensive but it should include key goals and objectives.

2. **Do the research.** The Department of Commerce is an excellent source of information on foreign markets for U.S. goods and services. Know what's available and not available in terms of your product or service. Having lived in London, I knew that black people see very few products with their likeness on them, unlike here in the States, where we take it for granted. In London I searched high and low to find a black doll baby for my daughter, Kayla. Knowing that there aren't many providers of "mocha" products gave me a considerable business advantage and generated a lot of buzz. Start off small to minimize risk. Or consider a joint venture.

3. **Figure out how you will distribute your product.** You can open a company-owned foreign subsidiary, work with agents, representatives, and distributors, or set up joint ventures. Test the market if possible. Having a booth at the expo event for black women was a great way to gauge interest and price sensitivity for our products. We learned a lot and got great exposure. If you have a product, consider getting a small retailer in a key area to sell it at no cost to them in exchange for any feedback on the product. If you offer a service, consider setting up a small satellite office. That's what Richelle McKinsey of Chicago did with her staffing service. After years of providing personnel services for big clients like Morgan Stanley and Citibank, she began asking her contacts at these firms for the names of their UK counterparts. Using the name of the American manager as a reference, she began contacting them to let them know her business was opening shop in London. She had a built-in recommendation and most were willing to give her a chance. Before she leased any office space, she had three London-based clients.

4. **Learn how to set prices, negotiate deals, and navigate the legal morass of exporting.** Cultural, social, legal, and economic differences make exporting a challenge for business owners who have only operated in the United States.

5. **Look into government help.** The government has a big interest in boosting exporting, and centuries of financial innovation have made getting funding and getting paid easier than ever. One of the most popular sources of financing for businesses expanding overseas is the Export-Import Bank of the United States. The Ex-Im Bank, as it's commonly known, is an independent U.S. government agency that has helped finance

overseas sales of more than $300 billion in U.S. goods and
services since 1934.

6. **Beware of cultural differences.** Don't assume people every-
   where think the same way as Americans. Or black Americans.
   Or American Latinas. Use the Internet to learn about the
   culture of the country you are targeting. Check out competitors or homegrown companies that do what you do to see how
   they market themselves. Read local magazines and websites to
   catch up on local trends and interests and pick up on certain
   lingo and colloquialisms to perfect your marketing language.

Not long ago, while I was talking to my manufacturer in India,
he mentioned that his wife was pregnant and wearing our Mocha
Manual girl shirt. And then it hit me: There are brown faces in
India too! India has a population of over 1 billion people with
nearly 500 million women! Stay tuned . . .

10. Revise Your Business Plan

After you have fully researched all of the above growth strategies,
its time to write down exactly how you will implement these to
take your company to the next level in a revised business plan.
When you first start out, your business plan may be fairly simple.
They are a lot of small business gurus who tout the benefits of a
two-to-five-page starter business plan like the one in chapter 3.
But remember, a business plan is a breathing document. It should
change over time as your business grows, industry trends change,
or new marketing methods and growth strategies are discovered.
As you get ready to take your company to the next level, you
should have a more comprehensive business plan of fifteen to

twenty pages. A solid business plan conveys your business goals, the strategies you'll use to meet them, potential problems that may confront your business and ways to solve them, the organizational structure of your business (including titles and responsibilities), and finally, the amount of capital required to finance your venture and keep it going until it breaks even. And it should sing like Luther! Fat Luther. There are three primary parts to a formal business plan:

- The first is the *business concept,* where you discuss the industry, your business structure, your particular product or service, and how you plan to make your business a success.
- The second is the *marketplace section,* in which you describe and analyze potential customers: who and where they are, what makes them buy, and so on. Here you also describe the competition and how you'll position yourself to beat it using some of the strategies mentioned in this chapter.
- Finally, the *financial section* contains your income and cash flow statement, balance sheet, and other financial ratios, such as break-even analyses. This part may require help from your accountant and a good spreadsheet software program.

Within these three major sections there are seven key components:

1. Executive summary
2. Business description
3. Market strategies
4. Competitive analysis

5. Design and development plan

6. Operations and management plan

7. Financial factors

Contact your local SBA or SCORE office to get some free assistance with your business plan.

When you think big but plan properly for growth, you are well positioned to build a lasting business. Things will be going so well, you'll be thinking about leaving your job to take the full plunge into entrepreneurship. Great! But make sure you read the next chapter before you do.

CONSIDER YOUR EXIT STRATEGY

This is one key area where many entrepreneurs get it wrong, but once your business is up and running, planning for an exit strategy is critical. When you think about it, there are few things that you truly enter blindly without having any idea how you will exit; whether it's a sports stadium, airplane, movie theater, college, or job, "Where is the exit?" is an important and familiar question. It should be equally familiar with your business. You need to plan your exit and build your company's exit strategy with as much care, passion, and determination as you did your entry. As with all babies, both the adorable cooing sort and the business sort, you spend years preparing them to be independent and thrive on their own. Yet a recent study shows that nearly 73 percent of women entrepreneurs lack an exit plan for their companies. The cost of missing this key component is critical, as many women business owners may deprive themselves of thousands or millions of dollars.

The Center for Women's Business Research found that 85 percent of both men and women rank price as the most important factor in their decision to sell their business. Not surprisingly, women are more interested in the buyer's future plans for the business than men are. And over three quarters of women plan to retire after selling their business, while 22 percent plan to start yet another business! Even if you don't know when your exit plan will happen, it should be a part of your thought process and business planning.

Exit options include:

- Selling your company to another company
- Selling to a family member, friend, or employee(s)
- Selling shares to the public via an initial public offering (IPO)
- Closing your company and selling off tangible assets and/or patents

Like anything else, a business is only worth what someone is willing to pay for it. As you're building your business with an exit plan in mind, you need to run it differently than you would as an entrepreneur running the company yourself. A potential buyer would want copies of tax returns, earnings statements, profit-and-loss reports, and the like. You build a company in a way that makes it as profitable and attractive as possible, which is a great incentive to reduce expenses,

(Continued)

boost sales, and run your company efficiently. That also means building a company that can be run without you. For example, when you own and run the company you have day-to-day control of operations; when you are molding the company for sale you delegate to your managers.

WHEN YOU RUN THE COMPANY . . .	WHEN YOU'RE BUILD-ING FOR AN EXIT . . .
You weigh in on every hire	You are only involved in the hiring of senior staff
You review every invoice	You only review final invoices or delegate to an accountant
There's no formal record of company rules	You have a written employee manual, which every employee receives upon hiring

You will need procedures manuals for each area of your business so buyers will feel confident that systems are in place for every aspect of your business. At some point there needs to be a valuation, which is more than just a numbers game—there is value in an established customer base, a unique marketing method, or a brand image too. By working closely with your accountant and attorney you can get top price for your business.

Of course, there's an emotional attachment to your business. There's no point starting a passion-centered enterprise if you don't care for it and feel for it personally. And then after years of building your business, nurturing it during good times and bad, it can be difficult to let go even if there is a sizable offer on the table. But in any relationship, love should not be blind. If you are overly attached to your business emotionally, it can cloud your good business judgment and lead to a major blunder like selling your company six months too late or missing the boat altogether.

Mocha Mix
Getting to the Next Level

* * * * * * * * * * * * * * * * *

You have to come out of your business and its day-to-day operations so you can focus on marketing and growing your business. There is no other way to get to the next level.

— PHOEBE SIMPSON AND SHARON SHAHEED, sisters and co-owners of Piano Play (www.pianoplaymusic.com)

I found that "doing it all" was my biggest challenge in growing my business. When you start a business, you have to assume so many roles you can become over-whelmed. When I became overwhelmed, I lost interest. When you lose interest, you lose money . . . which isn't good for business. When you delegate properly, your business can really grow.

— SHAQUANDA SPIVEY, president of SOLUTIONS Drug Testing Services, LLC, New Jersey (www.solutionsdts .com)

Sometimes selling your business is taking it to the next level. There's a perception in our community that if we sell something to a white company that we have done a bad thing. We have to be proud of *Essence* being purchased by Time Warner, and we have to say, "Fantastic!" We were raised with *Essence* as our sanctuary, but sacrifices have to be made for it to become what it deserves to be. If someone wants to buy your company, this is not about black or white. Are they in line with what you believe? Are they passionate about you? That's what matters.

— LISA PRICE, founder of Carol's Daughter (www .carolsdaughter.com)

Don't be afraid to empower other people to be involved in realizing your passion and dream. Let others in. Otherwise, you'll never grow.

— GINA STERN, owner of D_parture Spa (www.departure spa.com)

THE MILLION-DOLLAR LADY

Sandi Webster, cofounder of Consultants2go, a full-service
temporary consultant provider to midsize business

*Sandi Webster knows a li'l sumthin' about turning tragedy into triumph. Prior to
9/11, she had worked her way up the executive ranks of American Express to the
director level, where she spearheaded the database marketing and new business
launches. But after 9/11, her World Trade Center office relocated to New Jersey;
then the layoffs began. But before the ax fell, Sandi, at the age of forty, took a
buyout with the plan of starting her own firm. In 2006, just four years after
launching, her company, Consultants2go, topped $1 million in revenues.*

*Sandi, a serious fireplug who was born in Jamaica and raised in Brooklyn,
always knew entrepreneurship was in her future. She didn't know exactly when or
where her business venture would appear, but she viewed every job she took as
preparation for that someday. That someday began to seem closer and closer
when she identified a serious industry "pain."*

*The AmEx department Sandi coheaded worked with a small budget. So
when they needed consultants for IT projects, they were forced to hire from big
consulting firms with equally big rates—upwards of $400 an hour. "Our bud-
gets were often blown before the work was finished," Sandi says. Then she and
her department cohead, Patty McKale, started to think outside the box, beyond
the marquee consulting firms. They started thinking about their own network of
talented consultants—former colleagues who left corporate America because of
maternity leave, sick parents, or burnout. "We started reaching out to people we*

knew and asking them to come in and freelance for us. It was a win-win for everyone," she says.

So when it came time to think about life after the corporate world, Sandi figured they weren't the only corporate department having this budget problem. They thought that if they could target midsize companies of $30 to $100 million in revenue that don't have the marketing budgets of Fortune 500 companies and offer them more cost-effective consultant options, there could be a big business there. In a few weeks, Sandi and Peggy formed Consultants2go. Peggy had a strong network of decision makers in the telecom industry, and Consultants2go was immediately hired for a project. First, Peggy and Sandi did the work themselves, and then they started hiring other consultants so they could grow the business.

Today, Consultants2go offers two services. They take on a complete marketing project for a company, handing it back completely finished, or they provide a temporary consultant when a VP or director is out on leave.

In the first year, overhead was very low because they worked out of their bedrooms—a small perk when your business is more intellectual capital than anything else. With $2,000 invested in upgrading their home business equipment, they were off and running. They earned $6,000 in the first year, $125,000 in year two, $253,000 in year three, and over $350,000 in year four. Sandi and Peggy were then accepted into the American Express Make Mine a Million-Dollar Business program, and the million-dollar milestone came the next year.

Sandi shares these tips for building your own million-dollar baby:

Plan, plan, save, save

Be financially prepared. A start-up will suck money for at least one year. While I was working earning a solid six-figure income, I saved religiously. I support my mother, who lives with me, and I've raised my niece since her birth, so I have complicated financial responsibilities. But being a good saver gave me the extra cushion and confidence beyond the funds from the buyout I received from American Express to step out on my own.

Work your job

While in corporate America learn as much as you can. Get out of your comfort zone. If you don't know how to handle financials or manage people, get a job that will give you those skill sets. Better to fail on someone else's paycheck than your own.

Start small

Try to do it as a side hustle first to see if it works. As long as it's not a conflict of interest with your employer, don't leave your job until it's sustaining you or you have a clear plan on how it will do so.

Consider a partnership

Having a partner allows you to split yourself in two. You can double the efforts. Think of someone who has complementary business skills and similar core values. Work with a knowledge-able corporate attorney to create a legally airtight partnership agreement. And don't be afraid to talk about the things you hate to talk about, like "What happens to my stake if I die?"

Don't be afraid to step out of your business

One of my biggest lessons learned is that sometimes you just have to get out of your own way. Peggy and I were doing assignments, working on projects, and doing sales. We realized that we can't do everything ourselves. We decided to hire a salesperson and build a team. Once we made that decision, we were freed up to think about building the business.

Ask for help

We decided to ask for help—that was our steepest learning curve. But when we did, help came from amazing people and often from the least-expected sources. Also, join women's business groups, networking organizations, and your local chamber of commerce.

In the end, you just have to do it

It's good to start small and test the waters, but eventually you have to take the plunge. You have to make a decision to just do it.

CHAPTER EIGHT

Take the Leap: How to Transition from Employee to Full-Time Entrepreneur

Life is either a daring adventure or it's nothing.
—*Helen Keller*

We've spent all of our time talking about your side-hustle business, with the end goal of turning that side hustle into a profitable business. By following the guidelines and strategies outlined in the previous chapters, you should be well prepared to do that. But when your business grows, it will need more and more of your time. Eventually, you will have to think about leaving your full-time or maybe even part-time employment to focus on your business full-time.

Transitioning from employee to full-time entrepreneur is a biggie. This is the moment that separates the men from the boys, the wannabes from the I-ams, the talk-about-its from the be-about-its. There are thousands of women with a side hustle, but becoming a full-time business owner catapults you into the elite ranks of pure entrepreneurs. That makes you an incredibly fearless individual who can stand in the face of fear, self-doubt, uncertainty, and insecurity and change anyway. To act. To step into your power. This is the whole reason why we start a business based on our passion. Because it is our passion that gives us the energy to go forward when everyone is falling behind. It's our passion that gives us purpose and provides us with the capacity to keep going when any reasonable person would stop. It's passion that is the ultimate driver of people and the source of all promise and possibility. Now is the time to realize that possibility. Now is the time to move forward. As Andrew Morrison says, TAN! Take action now.

Stop waiting for someone else's permission to move forward. Stop waiting for that someday scenario. Stop waiting for more data, more information, pie charts, or spreadsheets. Stop waiting for courage as if it is just going to show up on your doorstep one day. What you are about to do is not about starting a business. It is about creating a life. And only you can do it, by simply doing it.

And you start doing it today. The first challenge of a successful transition is learning to revel in change instead of hunkering down to defend yourself from it. You can prepare for it as best you can, but the ride will be bumpy. And exhilarating. And even when you think you are prepared, something unexpected will happen. Things will happen. Life will happen.

So while this chapter is designed to create a personal plan to cushion you for the leap, understand that in the leap, you will find out who you really are.

Of course you should strive never to leap without a cushion beneath you. If there's one thing that brings inspired, high-flying entrepreneurs crashing back to earth, it's imploding personal finances. Sure, there are loads of stories about women who just quit their job one day without a penny in the bank, used their credit cards to finance their business, and now run a successful company. It does happen. But it's very risky. And stressful. That is not the optimum environment to grow your business properly. To improve your chances of success as you transition from employee to entrepreneur, you need to harness your financial resources. At this stage of the game, your personal finances and your business finances are inextricably linked. So you need to have a good grasp on both areas. You cannot begin to think about a transition plan until your money situation is figured out—it doesn't have to be perfect, but you do need to get your money straight.

To plan for the future, your first goal is to create (at a minimum) a six-month savings cushion. You need a cushion for household expenses and a cushion to support your business. To create any sort of nest egg for down the road, you have to get control over your spending now. To start, declare a Financial Friday night, light some candles, and sit down with a piece of paper. It's time for some personal reflection. Honestly evaluate your spending habits and identify where your money is going. Are you living beyond your means and buying things you really don't need? Your first response may be no, but before you draw that line in the sand, take a deeper look. On your first sit-down, meet with yourself. What are you willing to sacrifice for your dream? Write it down.

Next, meet with your spouse/partner. Explain what you want to do (hopefully, he knows this by now). Show him your sacrifice list and ask if there are things he would be willing to forgo (a vacation, eating out, a luxury car) to support you in realizing this dream.

Then you, or you and your partner, should start keeping a spending journal for at least a week. Get a small notepad and for the next week write down every single thing that you spend money on. If you buy a soda in the vending machine at the office, write it down. Morning newspaper, lunch money, after-work drinks, gas, fast food—write it all down. After you do this exercise for seven days, you will have a better understanding of your actual spending habits. And I guarantee you that there will be an "I didn't know I spent that much on that!" moment. You will have to make some short-term sacrifices to step into the life you crave. Before you make your next purchase, ask yourself if it will contribute to getting you closer to your goal or take you further away from it.

Create a Personal and Business Budget

With a clear idea of your actual spending, sit down with the budgeting worksheet on pages 276–278 to figure out your monthly income and expenses. Successful business owners understand the importance of a budget and follow it faithfully. Do you know how much money you're bringing in each month and how much is going out? Budgeting doesn't have to be unpleasant or difficult, and if you don't know where to begin, there is a multitude of helpful resources and articles on the Internet to get you started at no cost. Consider working with a financial planner if you have extensive credit card or other debt. Paying down credit cards and boosting your credit score will be key for getting funding down the road.

After you've completed your personal budget, look at your business finances. Is your company earning money yet? Are earnings outpacing expenses? If you've been following the steps outlined in the previous chapters, it should be. On the other hand, there are some types of businesses where you have to go full-time for it to really work. Or give it more time to grow. Look over your business budget. Based on how much the business is already earning, is there enough to support the business and make a contribution to your personal expenses?

ACTION PLAN

Review your income and expenses with a new perspective. Go back to your and your partner's sacrifice list. What can you do without? Can you scale down to basic cable, start brown-bagging your lunch a few days a week, change to a cheaper cell phone plan, or cut entertainment costs?

Find your floor. If you are in "make it happen" mode, what is the least amount of money that you can live comfortably on each month? Remember, I said sacrifices, not self-deprivation. A spending diet is like any other diet; if you completely deprive yourself of the things you love, you will only fall off the wagon and binge later. When you get a number that is comfortable for you and your family, write it down. This is your magic number. Then create a new budget based on this spending goal.

Do the math. Take your magic number, the number you can comfortably live on with some adjustments, and multiply it by six; this is how much you need to cover yourself for six months. This is your savings goal. Now go back to your current income. Subtract your new monthly spending limit (your revised budget after the agreed-upon sacrifices and cutbacks). The money left over will go toward your savings stash. **Your Current Income – Your New "Make It Happen" Spending Plan = Potential Savings to Put Toward Your Cushion**

Once you know how much you can save each month, you can figure out how long it will take you to build your six-month savings cushion. To get this number, divide the number needed for your six-month cushion by the amount you can now save each month.

If your savings goal seems too far off, don't be discouraged. First, you have to save smart with the money that you do have. Put your saved funds into a high-interest savings account (www.ingdirect.com or www.hsbcdirect.com offer good options). Then we need to start looking for cash in other places.

Look for Cash Elsewhere

Your house: Could you refinance your loan or get an equity line of credit?

Banks: Could you take out a small personal loan? You're more likely to get a loan when you have a job. Most people mistakenly wait until they are self-employed and then try to get a business loan, but then it is very hard to get funding.

A side hustle to your side hustle: If your savings are not enough yet you still want to leave your full-time employment, maybe there's something else you can do part-time to earn money. You can work on your business during the day and then get a part-time job at night. The extra income can help carry some of your business and personal needs.

Your partner: Would he be willing to "sponsor" you by taking on a second job or working overtime for a few months to help keep the finances afloat?

Your business: Do you have a product or service that can be presold so that you know the business has money before you leave your job? In one of my favorite books, *The Millionaire Maker* by Loral Langmeier, Loral talks about working with a family that realizes that their hobby of building custom go-carts is a moneymaking business they never even considered. With Loral's coaching, the family presold a custom go-cart online for $40,000 without even buying one part! Similarly, I met a woman in Los Angeles who started her children's clothing line by going to boutiques with a minicatalog of digital samples of her goods. A graphic designer with extensive Photoshop experience digitally imposed the designs on pictures of plain white T-shirts (I've also used this method successfully online with the Mocha Manual). This allows you to have a digital sample without incurring the cost of actually producing a shirt. She then went door-to-door with her catalog and sold preorders for the next season without spending much money. The money she received from preorders went toward producing the goods.

Friends and relatives: Ask friends and relatives to support you with monetary gifts or loans. Gifts are preferable. And I don't care if it's your sweet, kindhearted granny with her rocking chair and crocheted blanket, always get any agreements in writing and make sure the loans are set up with proper security, terms and conditions, and a repayment schedule. Host a fund-raising party in your own honor. Ask loved ones for donations. Even if they cannot donate monetarily, perhaps they can contribute services. After I asked for help, my friends and family gladly donated babysitting time to free me up to write this book and do the necessary traveling to run my business so I wouldn't have to pay for extra child care. I started calling people with dates that I needed help with and asking for commitments, and pretty soon the calendar was booked.

Your employer/former employer: Is it possible to still work for your company after you resign as a freelancer, consultant, or subcontractor? If you know you are highly valued for your skill with certain aspects of your job, from creating PowerPoint presentations to organizing conferences or events, can you ask to be hired just to do these tasks? Even if just temporarily, until your replacement gets up to speed? It may not be time to ask just yet (you don't want to let your plans to leave be known too soon), but think about it. Keep your ears open to learn if any similar arrangements have ever been made in the past.

Continue to brainstorm ways to earn extra money or save money. You know your grandma taught you how to make a dollar out of fifteen cents. After you figure out the finances you are ready for the next phases—the phases of actual transition.

A good transition plan takes time. Not that you shouldn't have an urgency about stepping into your entrepreneur life, but you can show your urgency by how quickly you cover the details of the plan, not by skipping them.

Phase One

Work your money plan. This is the most critical part of the plan. Stay focused.

Do your company reconnaissance. Before you get ready to resign to find time for your business, look at other ways to get some temporary time off first. Check your employee manual. Does your company offer paid or unpaid leave? This can give you one to three months to test the waters of full-time entrepreneurship. And you still have the security of your job waiting for you. Read all the fine print, including any terms and conditions that may require you to remain in your position for a set period of time after the leave.

Your company may also offer flextime schedules, from reduced workweeks to job sharing. Deneen Robinson of Deesignz Web and Graphics Studio (www.deesignz.com) in Indiana worked this company perk during her transition. After twenty years in corporate America, Deneen was quite skilled at navigating company policies and making the most of her corporate connections. At one point in her career, she supported eleven executives, handling everything from their schedules to their PowerPoint presentations. As a result, she became a multitasking expert: "If I learned how to be a one-woman show for these managers, I figured I could be a one-woman show for myself." Of all the responsibilities of her job, she really enjoyed the desktop publishing work. As a more creative outlet for these skills, she started preparing funeral and wedding programs at home for family and friends. To learn new skills, she took classes at night, which allowed her to do more graphic design work. After a few years, the busy job, demanding side hustle, and class schedule got the best of Deneen. She requested a compressed workweek—one of the flextime work arrangements offered by her company. She came in earlier every day in exchange for Fridays off. Then she compressed her workweek even further to have two days off. This was a great strategy for her to find more time for her business while keeping the benefits of her job. Can you reduce your workweek? Even if it involves a pay cut, it can be worth it. Start researching what your company offers.

What about unused sick or vacation days? Will you get paid for them after you quit or will you lose them? If you will get paid for these days, you may want to save them up so you can fatten your final paycheck. If you will lose them, start strategically planning how you will use these days to further your business. If possible, take your weeks off in one shot, giving you an uniterrupted, extended block of time to work your business.

I'm not officially endorsing this strategy, but my girlfriend, who shall remain nameless, orchestrated time off for elective surgery. For years, she wanted to have her bunions removed. And since her job required her to stand on her feet for several hours, it was the perfect type of procedure that would allow her to recover at home without too much pain while giving her at least three weeks off. In that time, while sitting in her bed with her feet up, she polished off a business plan, applied for trademarks, researched like mad, and put her business in play for her transition three months later.

What about tuition reimbursement or free courses through your company? Are there courses in business, time management, or leadership that would benefit your business that you can take advantage of as an employee?

Start researching health insurance. Health insurance is a major concern for the self-employed. About 24 million American small-business employees and their families are uninsured, according to a study by the Kaiser Family Foundation.

If you're lucky, your partner can add you to his health insurance (make sure to find out the exact cost and add it to your budget). Use various websites such as healthinsurancefinders.com and www.ehealthinsurance.com to comparison-shop for health insurance. Consider joining a trade association like the Freelancers Union to get prenegotiated group rates. And don't just investigate the price; look into the fine print of the policy. Check for warnings about preexisting conditions that may prevent you from getting coverage with that provider. I've seen Michael Moore's movie *Sicko,* so I know it can be tricky.

You may have heard about COBRA. Don't worry, it's not a snake, though it can bite. The Consolidated Omnibus Budget Reconciliation Act (COBRA) is a federal law that requires employers to allow departing workers to buy health insurance through the employer's group plan. For the first eighteen months after you leave your employer, you may elect to continue to receive coverage in your employer's group plan at your expense.

But you may be surprised at the cost of the monthly premiums. COBRA coverage can run $500 a month for a family and over $200 a month for an individual. My COBRA cost would have been over $900 for myself and two children in New York! Shop around.

Either way, figure it out. Don't skip health insurance. You can get a tax break for your pain. As a self-employed individual, you can now deduct 100 percent of your health insurance premiums. This is particularly good news because it is a so-called above-the-line deduction, which means that you can take advantage of this deduction even if you do not itemize deductions on your tax return.

Plan for the future. We know your business is headed to million-dollar status, but you don't want to forget about a retirement plan. Plus, if you're smart, you'll have a stash from the 401(k) at your current job that you will need to transfer. One of the best options for the bossless masses is the simplified employee pension—referred to as SEPs or SEP-IRAs. These are generic retirement plans that allow you to contribute and deduct up to 20 percent of self-employment income (25 percent of salary if you're an employee of your own corporation). However, the percentage can be varied each year, so lower amounts (or nothing at all) can be contributed when you turn out to be starved for cash. The maximum dollar contribution is $45,000 per year. SEPs are great for procrastinators because they can be opened up as late as the extended due date of your income tax return. Finally, SEPs are simple. It literally takes only minutes to get one started—usually with no charge—with a bank, brokerage firm, or insurance company. No annual government reports are required, and ongoing administrative expenses are nil.

Phase Two

Back to Business. You've settled into your reduced spending budget. Credit cards are being paid down. Your savings are on auto pilot. Now it's time to give your baby some more attention. Continue shoring up your marketing plan. Make sure you have your highly detailed marketing budget. This will likely be the biggest expense for your business, so you should try to do as much as possible while you have a job. Have you thoroughly investigated the costs of advertising, promotional cards, retaining a publicist or PR firm, or whatever else you plan to pursue?

How's your team-building coming along? Do you have your accountant and attorney on board? Have you included money for them in your ongoing business budget? Remember, there's the cost of retaining an attorney—which can be a considerable up-front lump sum—and the ongoing cost of keeping them around.

You want to leave your job with your business at a strong point or at the launching point. Complete as many research and administration projects as possible.

Be an entre-employee. Start looking at your job through the lens of your business. What can you take from your job to help further your business? And I don't mean paper clips, Post-its, and file folders (okay, maybe I do, but not only that). Think about skills you can use from web design, PowerPoint, Excel, or QuickBooks. Is there a formal training class you can sign up for or an in-house expert you can ask to teach you a few things in exchange for a free lunch? Plan strategic relationships and coffee and lunch dates with people in accounting, payroll, and marketing, and with the sharpest administrative assistant in the joint. Make nice with anyone with a skill you can learn or learn from. Let them talk about what they do and how they do it well. Take mental notes. Start looking at your workplace as a veritable learning feast; it's your job to suck everything from everyone you can.

And don't forget about clients, key relationships, and contact information. Would a referral from a senior executive be helpful in your business? Your job may allow you certain access to people, data, or skills. Make a list of the things you want to take from your job and create a plan to get them!

Phase Three

You're in the home stretch.

Recheck your savings goals. How close are you to your number? Make adjustments where needed in your financial plan. How's your credit score? After months of paying down credit cards, consider applying for an increased credit limit.

I. **Start developing a personal relationship with the managers where you bank.** When you visit the bank, dress appropriately and be friendly. After a few visits, ask to meet the manager. Mention that you're a longtime customer and local business owner. I'm a suburbanite and a big fan of the drive-up teller. It's so convenient! But as I moved closer to becoming a full-time business owner, I made a concerted effort to go into my local branch, say hello, meet the branch manager, and see and be seen, as they say. It's paid off handsomely in reducing fees, upgrading my accounts, and getting financial advice, plus I get a real "Norm" like kick out of walking into the bank and everybody knowing my name.

2. **Start dreaming about a quit date.** Are bonuses coming up? You'll want to wait until after that. Any major work projects you want to complete in a show of goodwill? When you've made a plan, put the date in your calendar or PDA. Then start thinking backward about the things you need to do before you leave your job.

Don't forget that how you quit is just as important as when. Though two weeks' notice may be an industry standard, it may create more goodwill to give more time, offer to assist with training your replacement, and tie up any loose ends.

When you quit can be important too. At my job, I learned during my company reconnaissance phase that if you quit early in the month, your health coverage would be paid for the entire month. That was one month of free health coverage.

3. **Get fully focused on your business.** If there are client meetings to be had, get started; if you need to ramp up sales, then review your marketing plan and execute. This is the time to find your hustler spirit.

4. **Plan an inexpensive emancipation celebration with close friends and families.** This is a great way to launch your new lifestyle and show your support network that you're stepping into a new career path with confidence.

5. **Expect the butterflies.** This is a very big step! You will have anxiety. You will second-guess yourself. Review your plan. Know that you are prepared. Recommit to a new life.

This is your time to leap. Take with you the strength of all the women before you who endured and persevered to turn their passions into profitable businesses. You can too! As you get ready to make the leap, never confuse falling with failing. And remember, it is only by hurtling through the void that we learn how to fly!

Mocha Mix
Stepping Into the Life of an Entrepreneur

* * * * * * * * * * * * * * * * *

Be sure to have a plan. Then work your plan.
— MARSHA BURNETT, president of Musical Directions,
  New York/Detroit/Los Angeles/London (www.musical
  directions.com)

My advice is to have a minimum of six months of your
income saved *before* leaving employment.
— SHARON SAULS, CEO of SKY Neurological Rehabilitation, Maryland (www.skyneurorehab.com)

I worked every corporate perk. I took advantage of reduced workweeks and then took a three-month "personal development" unpaid leave. This allowed me to try
out being a full-time entrepreneur.
— TRACY COLLINS, president of Gold Star Productions,
  Burlington, New Jersey

Don't quit your day job *yet*! Make sure your ducks are
lined up. Have your team in place. Once you leave that
nest it's a different ballpark. Make sure you have planned
financially for every possible scenario.
— KAREN TAYLOR BASS, president and CEO of Taylor
  Made Media, New York (www.taylormademediapr
  .com)

Once you've done the prep work, the only thing left to do is TAN: Take Action Now. Start small. Start slow. Start now. Now is the time.

— ANDREW MORRISON, founder of Small Business Camp, New York (www.90dayplan.com)

If you have a job you *can* still have a business. I was entrepreneurial within the company. However, never do your personal work at your job. You also have to prioritize and be super-organized.

— HARRIETTE COLE, president and creative director of Harriette Cole Productions, New York (www.harriette cole.com)

An exit strategy is important so that you can time yourself. Timing is the key. All your hard work will pay off. It may not seem like it at the time, but it will happen.

— TAMI REED, CEO of In the Pink Productions, Atlanta (www.talkingwithtami.com)

THE FASHIONISTA

Toni Scott Grant, president of Scott Phree, Inc. (www.scott phree.com), an online fashion boutique

If you ever meet Toni Scott Grant you will first be struck by her energy. She is like a chocolate Energizer bunny. Whenever you meet someone with such enthusiasm, especially when that someone is a wife, stepmom, full-time student, and entrepreneur, you have to ask, Where does it come from?

"I absolutely love the art of fashion," Toni always says. That unadulterated love has helped her overcome serious business setbacks, having to start over, struggling to get funding, and losing her biggest cheerleader—her mom—after leaving her career in New York to return to Houston and care for her.

Toni spent nine years in the fashion industry, working as a celebrity stylist dressing the likes of Snoop Dogg, touring with Timbaland, and outfitting Jessica Simpson and the ladies of The View, *but she always wanted her own thing. She was a side-hustle queen, working as a fashion stylist and then taking office jobs in corporate America while back in Houston, all the while keeping her eyes on becoming a full-time businesswoman.*

She says that in retrospect, the bigger plan was for her to learn more first. For two years she worked as a showroom manager for a women's clothing company, acting as the go-between for any fashion editor or stylist who wanted to view the line or pull clothing. In that position she learned all the elements of fashion, retail, and management, and made valuable contacts—resources and skills that were critical to her future success.

Toni's story is like those of so many side hustlers turned entrepreneurs—slowly and methodically building, getting back up after emotionally draining setbacks, but maintaining an unwavering determination to see it through.

Toni shares her tips for growing a side hustle with style:

Research, research, research

It took me three years of research and online shopping to get my feelers for exactly how an online store could work and figure out what I would like to carry in my own store. The vendor research took another two years—including Internet research, going to the Magic retail conventions in Las Vegas (each season), and going to Los Angles and Dallas for other major trade shows. While working for the clothing company, I was able to gain a lot of contacts and I knew exactly what I was going to do while working there, so I saved each and every contact that we used for marketing, research, and manufacturing.

Manage your time wisely and stay focused

I have literally had to tell myself, "You just can't do it all!" I set my PDA and Outlook calendar with daily reminders and date tracers so that my time is wisely spent and managed effectively. Yet there are still times when certain to-do's fall through the cracks. The best advice is to always prioritize. Learn the power of *no* and keep the main thing the main thing. Your focus is very important; if it is off-kilter just a tad, you can lose the race.

Follow a "three-F" mantra

My three-F mantra is "family first, financial growth, and focus." I also have a three-P mantra, which is "perseverance, patience, and personality." You'd be surprised at how far it will get you!

Never underestimate the power of networking and the "likeability" factor

Networking is probably 70 percent of my business, so of course it is very important. There is also a "relatability" and a "likeability" factor in this business that can make or break a sale. This also applies to almost anything that you do. When I network, I'm essentially selling myself. Once I've won the heart of the customer, I could pretty much sell her anything and she would buy it. The trick is making your customers feel like they are a part of your company without them ever meeting you.

Always overcome heartbreak and setbacks

I'll never forget the day my heart was truly broken. We received a rejection letter from the Miller Brewing Company Urban Entrepreneurs Series Business Plan Competition. I just knew I had a good chance to win. I was in the semifinals. My husband and I worked diligently on a solid business plan that we knew would win us the $20,000 prize, or at least the $5,000 third-runner-up prize. We worked day and night, hours on end, while we were both holding down day jobs and I was going to night school. We even enlisted my mother-in-law, who is a CPA, to do the numbers for our projections. And then the letter came—we had lost. I was devastated. I cried. I wouldn't take phone calls from family members asking if we won, and I refused to leave my room. My husband came home that evening with a beautiful card and at the end, in his own words, it said, "Honey, I know yesterday was tough and I know all too well how bad we needed that seed money, but guess what? There will be more days to come such as yesterday, but like a duck who escapes the water and shakes it off of his back, that's what you have to do. Hey, if it were that easy to be in business, everybody would be doing it." And with that, I continued on. That card is planted in my office and whenever a bank says no or a customer is yelling about their order being lost in the mail, I read that card, smile, and prepare for a better day.

Get yourself out there

I write a regular fashion blog, and we also mail out membership cards to our "elite" customers and offer rewards and discounts each time they shop on our website.

Recognize the power of *Free!*

My experience as a showroom manager for a clothing line in New York taught me that what really works with women is *free* items. I have applied that to my own business. Even with a small budget, you can do a lot by giving away a little.

Go the extra mile

We started a new "mobile service" for our local customers. We deliver to their home at no charge. They receive the same service and packaging, but in a matter of a couple of hours after their order has been received and filled. We also offer free styling assistance from style experts. This gives customers a chance to e-mail questions they have about piecing together an outfit and even if they didn't purchase the clothes from us, we will still offer the free advice via our toll-free number or e-mail. It's just something extra to connect with customers and offer them personalized service.

Always plan for the future

The next phase is to definitely get sponsors and maximize brand awareness with regional fashion shows. We would also like to have a physical store. We have already researched how much we need and possible funding options like bank loans or SBA loans. We have already been rejected twice for loans. But we will continue to try until we get a yes.

Don't overwatch the competition

I watched the competition a lot in the early days, but I've slacked off a great deal because I find it distracting. There will never be one oak tree; each tree is different, and that's how I look at the competition. I focus on what makes my company unique and what makes a customer want to shop with me as opposed to the competition.

Surround yourself with greatness

Align yourself with people who are like-minded and in the same field so you can get sound advice on business matters and overcoming personal and business hurdles. Find a mentor who is reaching for or has achieved the exact same goal that you are striving toward.

Everything is a learning opportunity

Always consider the possibility that you may not be successful your first time, but it will most certainly lead to another door opening. Be willing to pay the price for successes and failures, using both as learning experiences.

CHAPTER NINE

Getting Personal: Take Charge of Your Business and Your Life

Nothing will work unless you do.

—*Maya Angelou*

Okay, by now you've matched your passion and purpose to a viable business idea, figured out how to market and sell it, and even learned how to plan for the big leap into entrepreneurship. You're all set, right? No! There's one more area that's critical for business success, and that is properly managing your personal relationships.

A business is like a baby. You nurture it, you spend all your time thinking about it, and just like a real baby, it forever changes the nature of your relationships with others. When you're supporting a baby, you may have to sacrifice those lunches with your girlfriends at the trendiest (and most expensive!) spots. When you're growing a baby, your late-night chat time with friends and relatives is often replaced by work time. And your date nights with your sweetie may quickly become a fond memory. There are other people in your life, and they too will be affected by your entrepreneurial venture. Balancing all those relationships is key to your business and personal success.

The irony of the entrepreneurial life is that so many women start a business in search of some sort of work-life balance. They want more autonomy, more hours with their loved ones, etc. The reality is that often, particularly in the early stages of "birthing," you spend more hours with your baby then you ever imagined. You may work longer and harder than ever before. The only consolation is that you're doing it in your pj's, or while sitting down with your kids, or at least within earshot of them.

Most of the time you're overcommitted, overexhausted, and overextended. That's how I find myself most days. But somewhere in the tiredness and the forty-to-sixty-hour workweek is freedom. Freedom in knowing that when you have completed those sixty-plus hours you are closer to reaching your personal goals—not making money for someone else. You are an entrepreneur because you crave freedom. The corporate confines don't fit with your vision for your life. You want the time you live to be your time.

The problem is, in our quintessential search to squeeze out a few more hours every week, we can end up straining our relationships with those who aren't involved in our adventures. During the course of interviewing women for this book, I was struck by how many paid a high price for their entrepreneurial success. Several sisters lost someone precious while building something dear. For some it was a marriage mate, fiancé, relative, or irreplaceable sister friend. Sometimes we lose touch with those closest to us and forget. And sometimes we think someone else in our life is on board when in fact they are not.

Starting a business can cause financial strain, particularly if you decide to leave full-time work to pursue it. Even if you are working, extra money that may have gone to family vacations, lavish holiday spending, and I-love-you trinkets may now be flowing to your venture. Everyone is affected. Sacrifices are being made by all. And financial strains are the leading relationship killer. Some women are able to recover, repair the damage to their relationship, and, with hard work, make a fresh start. Others are not.

Your Man

Somewhere in the fifth year of my second marriage, after two children and life on two continents, it became abundantly clear to me that my husband, despite his affirmations otherwise, was clearly not on board with my life plan. It was one of those moments that crept up on me slowly, like a warming sensation, except it was chilling. It was the day I stopped listening to his words and actually listened to his actions. It was about not who he said he was but the person his actions revealed. At the time, I had a demanding job that required a one-and-a-half-hour commute each way and I was building the Mocha Manual Company after I put the kids to bed, from about ten P.M. to two A.M. most nights. In retrospect, I'm sure that in many areas I was an absent wife, but I thought we had a mutual understanding that it was a short-term sacrifice for the greater good—most important, my being home with our children. For years, I wanted out of the long commutes to Manhattan, marginal hours with my children, and leaving my children's care in the hands of a nanny. So in between my long hours and sometimes a stressed-out short temper, I secretly put three "sex night" reminders in my phone every week, I got up early to cook dinner in the morning on Wednesdays so he wouldn't have to eat "nanny food" all week, managed to whip up a respectable Sunday dinner, and eked out a date night every now and then—always thinking I was doing a good job. I did sense a distance growing between us, and like many women, it was one more thing on my to-do list that I didn't have time to address. All in all, in retrospect, what I didn't have time for was the ego work. Underneath my husband's cocksure, confident appearance and demeanor was a level of insecurity I had never seen before.

Ladies, most men have egos. You know your man better than most others. But the truth is that there are centuries-old ideas about a man's role as protector, provider/hunter, and procreator. Instead of instilling pride, many psychoanalysts feel these norms have now become a trap for black men who can't fulfill all these roles as they would like to. Instead, they may seek an ego boost elsewhere or end up secretly depressed or acting out in their relationships.

Experts say part of the problem is the ambivalence many men have about what they really want in a partner/mate. Tiy-E Muhammad, a psychology professor at Clark Atlanta University, offered this view in an *Ebony* magazine article on black male-female relationships. "Modern-day men enjoy having an independent woman," he says. "Most men will say, 'I want a woman who's got it going on.' But after the relationship has begun, those same men will now want that woman to submit and be a part of his vision and his dream. He will want to be the dominant figure in the relationship in order to feel whole."

Deneen Robinson, who launched her own graphic design studio, had a similar experience. For years she was happily married with a stepson and a lovely house in New Jersey. "My husband started out as very supportive, but as the business grew and required more time he became jealous and withdrawn. My stepson was a big part of the business; he worked with me, but my husband wouldn't get involved. As I spent more time with the business, the business became the enemy." Eventually, Deneen and her husband divorced. Ironically, the same business that came between them became Deneen's saving grace after her marriage failed. Her business gave her focus and a purpose that helped her heal emotionally during the difficult time.

Toni Scott Grant had a completely different experience with her husband. "My business actually had a very positive impact on my relationship with my now husband, who was my fiancé when I started my business," she says. "He supports me one hundred percent! Had it not been for my husband, who sat up with me until four A.M. on numerous occasions, fixing technical issues, helping with long hours of research, and assisting me with trial and error, I would not have had the focus or drive to continue. With every major setback, he has always said the right thing to help me pick myself up off the floor and get back in the game," she says.

That's what every woman needs and deserves when starting a business. But keeping that support in place requires effort on your part too. One thing I learned while writing this book is that women who keep their marriages and significant relationships intact while starting a business should win a special kind of entrepreneur of the year award. Alison Richardson and her husband, Patrick, who live outside of Chicago, know this well. Thankfully they were one of the couples that were able to bring their marriage back from the brink of failure by realizing just in the nick of time that their union was being slowly destroyed by years of unspoken fears and buried resentments.

Several years ago, Alison left her corporate job to start her own website business. In the early phases this was extremely time consuming. Patrick dutifully took on an increased share of the household chores and pitched in even more with their three-year-old daughter, after working eight-hour days at his office. But Patrick says Alison was emotionally and physically withdrawn. "We would be in the middle of dinner and she would be mentally someplace else," Patrick says. "We used to be able to talk about any- and everything, but our conversations increasingly focused on her business. I felt neglected and alone in our marriage."

The breaking point for their marriage came one Saturday night. "Alison and I typically set aside Saturday evening as our time to relax, reconnect, and talk about our dreams and plans. As I poured the wine, settled onto the couch, and got ready for our time together, Alison said she needed to do a quick update on the website. What she said would be a few minutes turned into an hour. I waited and waited. I'd had enough. It was the last five years repeating itself over and over again," Patrick says.

"That night I blew up at Alison for once again deciding to work instead of spending time with me. For years I had sacrificed my needs to this business, and the feelings of being ignored just got the best of me. I laid it all out. My bitterness and anger. She talked about her fears and frustrations," Patrick says.

"We finally told each other things we'd each been afraid to say for years for fear of driving the other one away. I didn't think we would make it through this evening," says Alison. But an amazing thing happened. "After the dust settled, we both we felt cleansed and free. For the first time in years, I could see clearly what I had been unknowingly doing to Patrick and our relationship."

Together Alison and Patrick made some necessary changes in their routine and communications. They set aside a time to respectfully share their frustrations before they turn into resentment. They each learned how to see things from the other's perspective and how to be more compassionate toward each other.

Alison and Patrick avoided becoming another marriage that caved in because of the pressures of entrepreneurship. One of the keys is being attuned to each other's needs. I'm constantly reminded of one of my favorite Chris Rock HBO specials, *Bigger and Blacker*. In one part, he talks about the Monica Lewinsky scandal and blames Hillary Clinton for the whole mess. He says Hillary knows her man's weaknesses better than anyone else, and she should have been there giving Bill his "medicine" for the greater good of the country. The lesson here: ladies, know your man's medicine! It may be an ego stroke, it may be sex, it may even be a small gesture like saying thank you, but whatever it is that keeps your man feeling good about himself and fully engaged with the plan, do give it to him! And make sure you get yours too!

In relationships that work—those that endure for decades—the individuals who make up the couple take turns allowing each other to be "boss," experts say. You don't have to be totally submissive, but sometimes you go along with what he wants to do, even if it's not exactly what you want, and he goes along with what you want to do, even if it's not exactly what he wants.

And, ladies, feel free to relinquish some control, especially on the home front, which many of us see as our dominion. "Just because he doesn't feed the baby or clean the kitchen exactly the way you would or make dinner exactly the way you would, you don't just take that away from him or degrade his approach," says one psychotherapist. When I was writing *The Mocha Manual to a Fabulous Pregnancy,* my husband's idea of making dinner was pizza with baked beans. Hey, I learned to go with the flow. "If you nurture him and show appreciation for the way he does things, you're showing him respect and building up that trust in the relationship," the therapist says.

Your business success is dependent on your having a strong support system, and if you are married or in a significant relationship, your man is a key component of that support system. In the same way that you would praise and recognize your employees, you need to do the same in your personal relationships. "I'll never forget when my husband said that he resented the fact that I always had time for phone calls, meetings, and lunches for my employees and business associates but never had time to talk to him," says Tamara, who runs an IT consulting firm in New Jersey. That was her wake-up call. She began rethinking how she managed the business of her life. At the end of the day, it won't matter at all if you have the most successful company in the world if you end up unhappy and unfulfilled because of the damage done to your personal relationships.

Melinda Emerson, president of Quintessence Multimedia, located in Upper Darby, Pennsylvania, knows that mixing love and business is potentially a slippery slope. "I was single when I started my business, but one year into it I got married. My husband had a job where he traveled a lot, so my being busy was often unnoticed. When I transitioned from a home-based to an office-based business, our roles sort of changed. In 2002 my business was growing at such a pace that I needed more professional help than I could afford. My husband decided to quit his job and work for my company. It was hard to cut it off when I got home. I had to make a special point to make sure that he was the leader at home and I was no longer the boss. My husband and I worked together for four years, but we don't work together anymore. We definitely sought other people's advice on keeping our relationship intact," Melinda says. "If you work with your spouse or partner, my advice is treat the office like work with clearly defined roles. Drive separately, and don't cross lanes."

If you haven't done so already, have a lengthy conversation with your man. It is critical to discuss everything, including finances, time management, child care, household chores, and the impact your decision will have on your marriage and the dynamics of your family. Listen carefully to everything he says. Listen carefully to the things he doesn't say. Put your agreements in writing and then stick to them. Try these ideas:

1. **Tune in to WII-FM.** Everybody listens to WII-FM, aka "What's in it for me?" You need to tune in to his station. Help him see how he benefits from your starting this business, from being at home with your children, to greater financial control down the road, to your eternal gratitude for helping you realize a dream. There may be financial benefits if you work from home and can reduce child care costs and write off some of your home office expenses.

2. **Have a weekly—or at least monthly—meeting with each other.** Schedule time for communication. This is different from date nights where you rekindle romantic feelings for each other.

3. **Let him know how he can help you.** Instead of nagging him, do your best to let him know how he can help you be successful. Ask him to honor your work hours and not call you at those times. You can also request some assistance with certain household chores so that you can have some extra work time.

4. **Draw the line.** I knew it was time to check myself when I started bringing my laptop to bed. Some of my friends bring their BlackBerry to bed. It doesn't make for a happy marriage when the wireless connection is stronger than the one with your husband. Have at least a few nights per week when work is truly turned off.

To Prenup or Not to Prenup

I'm a sucker for fairy-tale endings. And it has always been a special wish for me and my girlfriends that we all make the pages of *Jet* magazine as one of those old couples who have been married a hundred years and are still loving strong! However, I am also a realist and, unfortunately, a two-time divorcée. So I have to extend a few cautions to business owners who may be getting married or otherwise mixing romance with finance.

There used to be a time when prenuptial agreements were only for the rich and famous. But anyone who owns a business should at least consider a prenuptial agreement. Remember, you have spent time and considerable expense building your business. That's a major investment that you should protect like you would protect your house. Sure your boo seems all lovey-dovey now, but unfortunately things change, and you don't want someone trying to take your business.

Clearly, a prenup can be an emotional issue. And frankly, I have no good advice on how to start that conversation—except definitely don't do it during an argument and do not make it a trust issue. Bad idea. A prenup is nothing more than a written contract signed by two people before they're married. It can be used to accomplish many legal and financial objectives, but in general, couples use it to protect separate property, like your personal business, or define what's marital or community property in the event of divorce.

Typically, the agreement spells out exactly what each person brings to the marriage in terms of what they own (assets) and what they owe (liabilities), and then details how those assets and liabilities will be disposed of after separation, divorce, or death. It might also detail how any assets and liabilities acquired during a marriage (say, through an inheritance) will be disposed of after separation, divorce, or death.

A prenup doesn't have to be filed in court, but it does have general guidelines that should be followed for it to be effective (see appendix for helpful legal websites). It also needs to be signed by both of you and notarized.

Your Friends and Relatives

Black women are notorious nurturers, connectors, and overextenders. You probably have a laundry list of commitments, from church committees to school groups and sorority events. Not to mention you are the unofficial caretaker of some aging relative or the unofficial ATM and personal savior of some can't-get-their-life-together cousin. These are all noble ventures. However, as you build your business, your priorities and time allocations shift. If you don't set clear boundaries for all the people in your life, your time will no longer be your own. Instead, time will own you.

Take the time to explain to friends and relatives what you're doing and what is involved. I learned an important lesson here: I used to assume that people knew what I was doing. I didn't talk to my parents about the details of what running my business involves. When I would say to friends and relatives, "I'm so tired," and they would say, "Why?" in my mind I'm thinking, What an insensitive so-and-so. Don't they have any idea what it's like for me? And then I realized that, no, they really didn't. Most of your friends and family who are nine-to-fivers still see the fantasy side of entrepreneurship. They think you're home all day while they are in a stuffy office, and your life is gravy. Even while writing this book, I found myself explaining to dear friends and loved ones how much work, time, sleeplessness, and focus it takes to write a book. They didn't understand why I was so unavailable. One close relative even asked if she could bring herself and her three children to stay at my house over the entire summer! Meanwhile I sent my own kids away to my mother's house over the summer so I could write. My point is, sometimes you have to educate folks about the responsibilities, unending hours, and true nature of your new lifestyle. So when people ask, I speak in specific truths. "I'm tired because I was up to two A.M. fulfilling forty-two orders on my own." Or "I'm tired because I was up at four A.M. to argue with my manufacturer in India who screwed up my shirt order." Or "I can't talk right now. I have to write six thousand words in two days. And that's just one chapter." Giving others a glimpse of the realities of your life instead of keeping up the "I have it all together" façade can go a long way toward getting you genuine support from those who love you most and getting you more understanding from your friends and relatives. Here are some other ideas:

1. **Learn to say no, with no apology or explanation.** You can say it very nicely, if that makes you feel better. Inevitably, some of the people in your life will be surprised by the new you as you learn to protect your time. Eventually, they will have to give

you your props for how you handle the nonstop job of being a business owner, wife, mother, and chief caretaker. Teach them early and stay in control!

2. Try to incorporate your friends into your business schedule. There's no rule that says you can't mix work in with pleasure. For instance, Tanisha Blackburn from Atlanta, Georgia, goes to a lot of trade shows for her import/export business. When a trade show is in a fun city, like Miami, she tells a girlfriend to meet her there. "Sometimes I say, 'Get your plane ticket; the hotel is on me.' Inevitably, I get sympathy help lugging my stuff to the show, then they hang out on their own for a few hours, and we meet up at lunch or dinner for girl talk and evening shenanigans."

Your Children

I had a dream. I left my job to have more time to be with my children. The truth is, I have more time *around* or *in the presence of* my children. I don't know if that's necessarily a good thing. Yes, it's true that I spent a good portion of my summer sitting on the deck watching my children run around the yard. But it is also true that I was always there with my laptop, writing and checking e-mails, peeking out from behind the computer every five minutes for an obligatory "Gee, that's great, Kayla," or "Good job, Michael," as if on cue. I pretty much had a rotation of comments I would blurt out in an Old Faithful sort of way, so that my children would think I was engaged in their activities. Unfortunately, most times I was not fully engaged. And that does not make me very proud.

The truth is, most adults, even the hardheaded ones, will eventually understand the journey you are going through. Your man will understand. Your girlfriends and family will eventually understand. Your children, however, may not. And though you may have a husband who helps keep the household routine flowing, and siblings who pick up the slack caring for your parents, and friends who cover for you at missed church meetings, nobody, and I mean nobody, can keep the relationship strong between you and your children except you. Depending on the age of your kids, they likely couldn't give a rat's behind about the business you're starting; they just want to know that Mommy is there for them. Be vigilant to stay tuned in to your children's daily lives. If you lose communication with them, it will be very difficult to get it back. I'll never forget the day I overheard Kayla tell her father something very personal that she had not shared with me. I was heartbroken. But it was my wake-up call that I have to give her more quality time—time when I am completely and fully present to her and her life and not thinking about e-mails or saying I only have a few minutes or being rushed about things. In your entrepreneurial journey, always let your children know that they come first.

FIVE TIPS TO A HAPPY(ER) HOME

1. **Beware of the danger of working from home.** When you work from home, the workday never seems to end. There are simply too many things to do. Part of having good time management skills is knowing when to stop, when to leave work and begin doing your other roles in your family as the wife, mother, daughter, girlfriend, etc. Even when you work from home, you must be able to know how to keep your home life separate from your work life and ensure that there exists a balance between the two.

2. **Get organized.** You don't have time to waste. Being organized saves the precious time you do have and helps you squeeze out

more for your children and spouse. Have a family schedule and planner so that everybody knows when it is work time, when it is family time, and who's picking up whom this week from dance class.

3. **Don't mess with dinner.** No matter what, I stop and have dinner with my children every night. Even if dinner is bologna sandwiches, we eat together, no television, every night. This is my promise to my children and myself. Whether it's dinner or bedtime tuck-ins, create your own unbreakable rules for being with your children and partner.

4. **Talk to your kids about your business.** Involve them in what you're doing as much as possible. You may have grown up in a house where talking about money and business was grown folks' conversation. Remember, your business affects everyone around you, so let them be involved. Kids love to help. At age seven Kayla was fully in charge of labeling promotional cards for mailings, putting stamps on outgoing mail, and cutting ribbon (under my supervision) for packaging orders. She loved it! Christine Robinson of Long Island used to bring her son to work with her every day. She had a computer company, and from age nine onward her son painted or partially painted every warehouse they ever stored inventory at. "I talked to him about how we make money. And when he sold his computer to his third-grade teacher for a profit, I knew I had a future entrepreneur on my hands," she says.

5. **Explain to them about the short-term sacrifices the whole family is making and what the long-term payoff will be.** When I worked at *Essence*, every day Kayla would ask, "Mommy, can you please be home before dark?" Now remember, I had an hour-and-a-half commute, so that meant if I actually left the office exactly on time at 6:00 and did an O. J. Simpson sprint

through Penn Station, the earliest I could be in my house was 7:40. And I could count my actual 6:00 office departures on one hand! In the summertime, there was good chance I could do it, but with daylight savings time, forget it! Impossible. But every day it broke my heart to tell Kayla, "Mommy will try her best." So when I started on my transition plan, I explained to Kayla that I could be home nearly every day to meet her at the bus stop (this was her WII-FM, aka "What's in it for me?"), but I might have to travel more on weekends and she would have to clean her room more by herself because we let the nanny go to cut expenses (this one she didn't really like!). But she understood trade-offs. I explained there would be less eating out, less spontaneous shopping, and more of a budget. I asked her if she was willing to help out with some of these sacrifices so I could be at home more with her and her brother, Michael. Kayla was totally on board! Now she views our changed family lifestyle as a team effort.

You

Ah, now to the most incredible piece of this puzzle. You, the phenomenal visionary, determined dream chaser with go-getter instincts—all of these elements are coming together because of you. You are a very important part of your family. And you are a critical component of your business. Like any valuable business asset, you have to protect yourself. And by that I mean take care of yourself to ensure that you are around and healthy to see your vision to its fulfillment and drive your business to success. I know you know the drill—"find me time" or "you have to make time for yourself." People always say that to me, and I often bark back, "When? Just tell me when and how and I'll be there."

That's when the phone usually goes silent. I still dream of a lei-surely lunch with a girlfriend, reading a book solely for the en-joyment of reading, a relaxing manicure and pedicure (not the one that needs to happen in thirty minutes or else . . .), or my biggest fantasy yet: a midday matinee.

Well, the only way any "me time" is going to happen is if you schedule it—and even then it can be iffy, so consider it an impor-tant appointment that you need to keep. Put it in your calendar. Block it out even if you don't have a specific plan. Keep remind-ing yourself that you're worth it. I had a bad habit of missing meals and living on very little sleep, and then I started to tell myself I'm worth stopping and eating. I'm worth getting proper rest most nights, if not every night of the week. Remember, this is not an hour wasted, it is an hour invested in the company's most important asset—you!

YOUR SPIRITUALITY

In general black women are spiritual people. Even if you're a Bedside Baptist, you recognize a greater being (even if he comes to you through the television). This is an area that should not be neglected. So many women said that when their spirituality was out of whack everything else didn't work either. But when they put their spirituality in its proper high-priority slot, everything else worked out. Whether you turn to prayer, meditation, or quiet inner reflection, try to take a few minutes every day to quiet your thoughts and center yourself. Your mind will be clearer, your heart will be lighter, a weight will seem to be lifted off your shoulders, and your stress level will be reduced. Deneen Robin-son, of Deesignz Web and Graphics Studio, always says when you put God first, everything else will come into place. Even if you get your few minutes in the car en route to a meeting, turn off the radio, turn off your cell phone, and get present to your current state of affairs.

YOUR HEALTH

Stress is a killer. And quite frankly, black women have enough health odds stacked against them already. According to the Centers for Disease Control and Prevention, the leading causes of death for black women in the United States are heart disease, cancer, stroke, and diabetes. The risk factors for heart disease, the number one killer of black women, are obesity, lack of activity, smoking, high cholesterol, and hypertension. Do you have any of these factors in your life? The deplorable state of black women's health in this country has relegated black women to the bottom of nearly every health index compared to other women and, in some cases, when compared to black men. Too many black women are dying too soon and needlessly. Too many others suffer unnecessarily from preventable conditions.

The U.S. Department of Health and Human Services says that black women are less likely to receive health care, and that when we do, it's too late. I have a girlfriend who will drop everything to take her kids to the pediatrician. She will even drop most things to get her dog to the vet, but when it's time for her to go to the doctor she has every excuse to put it off.

Ladies, please, take control of your health, just as you take control of other things in your life. Without you, this journey doesn't work. There will be no entrepreneur for your business. No mate for your spouse. No mom for your kids. Make your health a top priority. Time to get your Fannie Lou Hamer on! The immortal words of the political activist, "I'm sick and tired of being sick and tired," have become a clarion call for black women today. To get back on track:

1. Commit yourself today to taking better care of your own health needs—physically, mentally, and spiritually. Don't let deadlines, jobs, child care, parent care, and everything else in your life delay your own care.

2. Make healthy living for black women part of your business mission. Where possible, incorporate a free blood pressure test or health screening into your business promotional and marketing plans.

3. Commit to being your sister's keeper when it comes to health, as encouraged by the Black Women's Health Imperative (visit www.blackwomenshealth.org). Make sure that the members of your personal sister circle are taking care of their health matters. Take a stand for yourself and those you love!

Mocha Mix
Words of Wisdom on Life Balance

* * * * * * * * * * * * * * * * *

Figure out something that creates a spiritual balance; you need to have a balanced life. Many women are very successful but extremely unhealthy. Find a balance.
— HARRIETTE COLE, president and creative director of Harriette Cole Productions, New York (www .harriettecole.com)

Mind your relationships; it doesn't cost anything to treat people like human beings. Learn to manage your emotions and, if necessary, get a therapist to help you.
— JINNIE ENGLISH, president of Chicago's High Achievers, Illinois (www.getting-better.net)

Hold firm to your belief system, whatever it may be. There will come times when things just don't make sense and you may even wonder if what you are doing is going to work. You have to just keep on believing!
— SHARON SAULS, CEO of SKY Neurological Rehabilitation, Maryland (www.skyneurorehab.com)

If you want the best life, you have to eliminate fear. Fear is the most destructive emotion. It impacts all major organs in the body. When you're afraid, cortisol is released and it's damaging to the body. People are operating all day long in this state and they end up with a compromised immune system.

— ANDREW MORRISON, founder of Small Business Camp, New York (www.90dayplan.com)

I wasn't making time for my prayers and I had stopped doing what I love—dancing. Things were off for me. So I started taking dance classes again, got rid of nervous energy, and started with heated yoga. It helped center me. Revisiting the Bible has brought calm to my life. Before, I worked all day and then again when I came home; now I simply come home. I take time to enjoy life. I can be even more grateful right now because I can take time to enjoy my blessings.

— ANDREA FAIRWEATHER, CEO of Fairweather Faces, New York/Los Angeles (www.fairweatherfaces.com)

I always remember this quote from a writer named Anna Garlin Spencer: "No book has yet been written in praise of a woman who let her husband and children starve or suffer while she invented even the most useful things, or wrote books, or expressed herself in art, or evolved philosophic systems." It helps me get my priorities straight.

— JOYCE DAVIS, founder of PowerFlow Media, Atlanta

Finding time for myself was the hardest thing to do. My health really suffered, I was cranky all the time. I realized that sacrificing sleep to get things done and staying up to all hours of the morning just didn't really work. The price to pay was very dear.

—ALICIA HOLMES, president of x station, an import and export business in Mechanicsville, Virginia

THE BRAINIAC

Sharon Sauls, president and CEO of SKY Neurological Rehabilitation, a full-service outpatient center for persons with
acquired or traumatic brain injuries, strokes, and other neurological conditions; SKY is the only black-owned company of
its kind in the United States. and the only freestanding facility in the state of Maryland with a stroke specialty accredita-
tion

*Sharon Sauls was building an impressive career in health care consulting, helping
large and small companies with business development, marketing, and other business practices so they could have successful companies. But in her mind, she always
knew she had the gift of leadership. Friends kept encouraging her to start her own
business. But she didn't have the outlet, the conduit to put her innate leadership
and business-building abilities to work. Later, through her consulting work, she
learned of neurological rehabilitation—a specialized therapy for persons who have
suffered strokes and other brain injuries. With strokes being so common in the
black community, Sharon personally thought of close relatives and friends who
would have had a much better recovery and quality of life if they had specialized
therapy.*

*Today, she has a million-dollar enterprise, including two flourishing centers
in Maryland that have worked with over a thousand patients and counting. She
began with a partner and five employees in 2002 and now has over twenty-five
employees. All this with a little help from her friends.*

Sharon shares her tips on building a strong business:

See it for yourself

I was talking to a dear friend of mine, who is also a very successful entrepreneur, and he said, "Sharon, you've been helping others with their business plans; you should establish yourself so you can get paid for it." Over time, other close friends who were acquainted with business ownership and successful leadership saw my potential, spoke it to me. But it wasn't until one day when I had a vision of my own success that it was real for me. Immediately, the tables turned. Everything that I was sharing with others about business development and leadership would now be applied to my own venture.

Get others involved in your mission

After accepting the vision, I immediately thought of who I'd ask to join me to work on the details of the plan. I reached out to a former colleague and career neurological rehabilitation therapist, Yvette Valiente, to ensure that the product was the best we could make it. She was an expert in the clinical model. I developed a professional advisory board that consisted of people with expertise in every aspect of the business—information systems, legal, ethical practices, medical insurance, workers' compensation, medicine, human resources, etc. Every time we thought of a resource that we needed, an advisory board member came to the rescue.

I planned a special meeting with those closest to me to share my vision and to request that they join me in prayer and ask God to bless the outline of the plan and give direction as we moved forward to develop it and work it.

Sometimes you have to ignore the rules

I went against everything that I had ever read about starting a business. I didn't have six months of my income saved before starting the business, and that is what I would advise others to have. I was consulting with an HMO at the time that would potentially introduce the services that my company would provide, so I saw a conflict. I knew that I needed to aggressively write and work the plan, so I quit my job.

Be prepared to make sacrifices

I could write a book about sacrifices. There I was, a single professional woman with a professional lifestyle—having only one income, working on a doctoral degree, living in a different state than my immediate family—deciding to forgo my steady income to work the plan. There were a lot of sacrifices. But the impact was invaluable. The things I took for granted became significant and things that I once valued so much became insignificant.

Get involved in the community

Business owners in the human services field must connect with people in order to be successful. My first strategy was to meet the who's who of the community where we decided to open our first center. I contacted the county executive's office, introduced myself, and asked who could help me connect with the key players in the county. I also scheduled meetings with health care professionals in the area who frequently see the patients who would need our services to let them know we were bringing the service to the area. We also met with organizations and associations that provided advocacy and support for the patients.

Celebrate milestones

I'll never forget the day we finally received funding for the project after several rejections. The next milestone was when we received the keys to our first facility and had the dedication and blessing. Then we celebrated our one hundredth patient, and five years later the one thousandth patient. Nothing cheers me up more than seeing patients graduate from wheelchairs to walkers and progress from one-word sentences to five-word sentences.

Learn from my mistakes

1. I should have downsized my lifestyle within the first twelve months of business plan development and start-up. The original launch date and actual launch date were approximately seven months apart.

2. I should have seriously considered the potential strain and implications of trying to grow a business with a partner who is married with young children.

3. I should not have promised start dates to the start-up team until funding was actually in the bank and not just promised.

4. I should not have offered staff titles until after six to nine months of working as a team so I could better note strengths and weaknesses and see how they related to their roles and responsibilities.

Always believe in yourself

There will come a time when things don't make sense and you wonder if it will really work. Just keep on believing!

Sample Documents

<hr>
SAMPLE PRESS RELEASE
<hr>

FOR IMMEDIATE RELEASE:

CONTACT:

Contact Person

Company Name

Phone Number

Fax Number

E-mail Address

Website URL

XYZ INC. ANNOUNCES WIDGET
TO MAXIMIZE CUSTOMER RESPONSE RATE

The headline is one of the most important components of the press release as it needs to grab the attention of the editor. It should be in bold type and a font that is larger than the body text. Preferred type fonts are Arial, Times New Roman, and Verdana. Keep the headline to 80 to 125 characters maximum. Capitalize every word with the exception of "a," "the," "an," or any word that is three characters or less.

<CITY>, <STATE>, <DATE>—Your first paragraph of the release should be written in a clear and concise manner. The opening sentence contains the most important information; keep it to twenty-five words or less. Never take for granted that the reader has read your headline. It needs to contain information that will entice the reader. Remember, your story must be newsworthy and factual; don't make it a sales pitch or it will end up in the trash.

Answer the questions "who?" "what?" "when?" "where?" "why?" and "how?" Your text should include pertinent information about your product, service, or event. If writing about a product, make sure to include details on when the product is available, where it can be purchased, and the cost. If you're writing about an event, include the date, location of the event, and any other pertinent information. You should include a quote from someone who is a credible source of information; include their title or position with the company and why they are considered a credible source. Always include information on any awards they've won, articles they've published, or interviews they've given.

Keep your sentences and paragraphs short; a paragraph should be no more than three to four sentences. Your release should be between five hundred and eight hundred words, written in a word processing program, and spell-checked for typos. Don't forget to proofread for grammatical errors. The mood of the release should be factual, not hyped; don't use a sales pitch as it will ruin your credibility with the reader.

The last paragraph before the company information should

read: "For additional information on [the subject of the release], contact name or visit [your website URL]." If you offer a sample, copy, or demo, put the information in here. You can also include details on product availability, trademark acknowledgment, etc. in this area of the release.

ABOUT <COMPANY>—Include a brief description of your company along with the products and services it provides.

- END -

At the end of the release, you need to indicate that the release has ended. This lets the journalists know they have received the entire release. Type "End" on the first line after your text is completed. If your release goes over one page, type "MORE" at the bottom of the first page.

SAMPLE BUDGETING WORKSHEET

INCOME

Take-home pay	_____
Take-home pay	_____
Other income	_____
Total income	_____
Fixed	_____

EXPENDITURES PROJECTED ACTUAL (+) OR (-)

Mortgage/rent	_____	_____	_____
Credit-card payments	_____	_____	_____
Home equity loans	_____	_____	_____
Car loan(s)	_____	_____	_____

TAXES NOT WITHHELD FROM PAY

His	_____	_____	_____
Hers	_____	_____	_____

INSURANCE PREMIUMS

Life	_____	_____	_____
Auto	_____	_____	_____
Home	_____	_____	_____
Health	_____	_____	_____
Other	_____	_____	_____

SAVINGS/INVESTMENTS

Vacation fund	_____	_____	_____
Emergency fund	_____	_____	_____
College fund	_____	_____	_____
Retirement/401(k)	_____	_____	_____

Investment fund   _____   _____   _____

Other   _____   _____   _____

   _____   _____   _____

Variable   _____   _____   _____

EXPENDITURES PROJECTED ACTUAL (+) OR (-)

Fuel and Utilities

Heating   _____   _____   _____

Electricity   _____   _____   _____

Telephone   _____   _____   _____

Water and sewer   _____   _____   _____

Household operation   _____   _____   _____

TRANSPORTATION

Automobile—gas
   and repairs   _____   _____   _____

Public transportation   _____   _____   _____

CLOTHING

His   _____   _____   _____

Hers   _____   _____   _____

Kids   _____   _____   _____

POCKET MONEY

His   _____   _____   _____

Hers   _____   _____   _____

Kids   _____   _____   _____

OTHER VARIABLE EXPENDITURES

Food and beverages   _____   _____   _____

Personal care
   (haircuts, etc.)   _____   _____   _____

Recreation,
    entertainment   _____   _____   _____

Medical/dental   _____   _____   _____

Charity   _____   _____   _____

Special expenses
    (tuition, alimony,
    etc.)   _____   _____   _____

Miscellaneous   _____   _____   _____

     _____   _____   _____

SUMMARY

Fixed expenditures   _____   _____   _____

Total expenditures   _____   _____   _____

Income minus
    expenditures   _____   _____   _____

Income minus
    expenditures over
    12 months   _____   _____   _____

APPENDIX

Accounting

QuickBooks Software

Website: www.quickbooks.intuit.com

Microsoft Office Accounting Express

Website: www.microsoft.com/smallbusiness

Accounting Coach

Website: www.accountingcoach.com

Accounting for Dummies by John Tracy (2008)

Accounting for Non-Accountants: The Fast and Easy Way to Learn the Basics by Wayne Label (2006)

Small Business Accounting Simplified by Daniel Sitarz (2006)

Books for Entrepreneurs

The Tipping Point: How Little Things Can Make a Big Difference by Malcolm Gladwell (2000)

The Seven Habits of Highly Effective People by Stephen R. Covey (2004)

The Complete Idiot's Guide to Starting Your Own Business by Edward Paulson (2007)

Ladies Who Launch: Embracing Entrepreneurship and Creativity as a Lifestyle by Victoria Colligan and Beth Schoenfeldt (2007)

Business Plans

Bplans

Website: www.bplans.com

How to Write a Business Plan by Mike McKeever (2007)

MiniPlan.com

Create a mini business plan free online.

MasterPlans: Professional Business Plan Writers

1231 NW Hoyt Street, Suite 305

Portland, OR 97209

Website: www.masterplans.com

SBA Business Plan Basics

Website: www.sba.gov/smallbusinessplanner/plan/
   writeabusinessplan/index.html

Business Networking Organizations

Center for Women's Business Research

1411 K Street NW, Suite 1350

Washington, DC 20005-3407

Phone: 202-638-3060

Fax: 202-638-3064

Website: www.nfwbo.org

Minority Business Network Services

Website: www.mbnet.com

Minority Business Development Agency

1401 Constitution Avenue NW

Washington, DC 20230

Website: www.mbda.gov/

National Association of Women Business Owners

8405 Greensboro Drive, Suite 800

McLean, VA 22102

Phone: 800-55-NAWBO

E-mail: national@nawbo.org

National Women's Business Council

409 Third Street SW, Suite 210

Washington, DC 20024

Phone: 202-205-3850

Fax: 202-205-6825

E-mail: info@nwbc.gov

Website: www.nwbc.gov

Service Corps of Retired Executives (SCORE)

SCORE Chapter I, District of Columbia

1110 Vermont Avenue NW, 9th Floor

Washington, DC 20005

Phone: 202-606-4000 ext. 287 or 800-634-0245

Fax: 202-293-0930

Website: www.score.org

U.S. Small Business Administration

Phone: 800-827-5722

E-mail: answerdesk@sba.gov

Website: www.sba.gov

United States Chamber of Commerce

Website: www.uschamber.org

Women's Business Enterprise National Council (WBENC)

1120 Connecticut Avenue NW, Suite 1000

Washington, DC 20036

Phone: 202-872-5515, ext. 10

Fax: 202-872-5505

E-mail: admin@wbenc.org

Website: www.wbenc.org

West Coast Operations of WBENC

Regional Director, West Coast

3579 East Foothill Boulevard, Suite 188

Pasadena, CA 91107-3119

Phone: 626-836-9288

Fax: 626-836-5709

Business/Entrepreneurial Publications

Black Enterprise

130 Fifth Avenue, 10th Floor

New York, NY 10011-4399

Phone: 212-242-8000

Website: www.blackenterprise.com

Business Week

Website: www.businessweek.com

Entrepreneur

Website: www.entrepreneur.com

Forbes

Website: www.forbes.com

Think and Grow Rich by Napoleon Hill (1937)

The One-Minute Entrepreneur: The Secret to Creating and Sustaining a Successful Business by Ken Blanchard, Don Hutson, and Ethan Willis (2008)

Financing/Venture Capital

BoldCap Ventures LLC

Boldcap Ventures LLC

969 Third Avenue, 4th Floor

New York, NY 10022

Website: www.boldcap.com

Capital Across America

Website: www.capitalacrossamerica.com/

FundingPost

Second Venture Corporation

7365 Main Street, Suite 324

Stratford, CT 06614

Phone: 800-461-5509

Website: www.fundingpost.com/

Isabella Capital

Isabella Capital LLC

1995 Madison Road

Cincinnati, OH 45208

Phone: 513-721-7110

Fax: 513-871-7150

E-mail: info@fundisabella.com

Website: www.fundisabella.com

Inroads Capital Partners

Website: www.inroadsvc.com

Key Bank: Key 4 Women

127 Public Square

Cleveland, OH 44114

Website: www.key.com/html/I<->5.html

McColl Garella

Website: www.mccollgarella.com

Milepost Ventures

Website: www.milepostventures.com/

OPEN from American Express

Phone: 800-519-OPEN (800-519-6736)

Website: www.open.americanexpress.com

For businesses with more than $1 million a year in revenue, call
866-690-4896 to hear about products designed specifically
for you.

Seraph Capital Forum

Website: www.seraphcapital.com

Small Business Administration Loan Programs:

Venture Capital

Website: www.sba.gov/womeninbusiness/wventurecapital.html

SBA Answer Desk

800-U-ASK-SBA (800-827-5722)

Answer Desk TTY: 704-344-6640

E-mail: answerdesk@sba.gov

Micro Loans

Website: www.sba.gov/services/financialassistance/sbapartners/
microloan/index.html

CAPLines Loan Program

Website: www.sba.gov/smallbusinessplanner/start/
financestartup/serv_caplines.html

Springboard Enterprises' Women-Capital Connection

2100 Foxhall Road NW

Washington, DC 20007

Website: www.springboardenterprises.org

Wachovia's Women Business Owners

Phone: 800-566-3862

Website: www.wachovia.com/small_biz/page/0,,447_624,00
.html

Wells Fargo Women's Business Services

Website: www.wellsfargo.com/biz/intentions/AfricanAm_
bus_svcs

Financial Planning/Personal Finance

Bridgforth Financial

1300 Lafayette East, Suite 3202

Detroit, MI 48207

Phone: 313-566-0026

Fax: 313-887-9546

Website: www.bridgforthfinancial.com

*Girl, Get Your Money Straight: A Sister's Guide to Healing Your Bank Account and
Funding Your Dreams in Seven Simple Steps* by Glinda Bridgforth
(2002)

Certified Financial Planner Board of Standards Inc.

1670 Broadway, Suite 600

Denver, CO 80202-4809

Phone: 303-830-7500

Website: www.cfp.net

Consumer Debt Counseling

1300 Hampton Avenue

St. Louis, MO 63139

Phone: 800-9-NO-DEBT

Website: www.cccsstl.org

Financial Planning Association

1615 L Street NW, Suite 650

Washington, DC 20036-5606

Phone: 800-322-4237

Website: www.fpanet.org

International Trade

Globe Trade

6807 N. Lakewood, Suite LL

Chicago, IL 60626 USA

Phone: 773-381-1700

Website: www.globetrade.com

Globe Women

666 11th Street NW, Suite 700

Washington, DC 20001

Website: www.globewomen.com

International Entrepreneurs Association

Holgrave House, 9 Holgrave Close,

High Legh, Knutsford, Cheshire

WA16 6TX Wales

United Kingdom

Phone: +44 (0)1925757887

Fax: +44 (0)1925758611

Website: www.ibizea.co.uk/

International Trade Administration
U.S. Department of Commerce
1401 Constitution Avenue NW
Washington, DC 20230
Website: trade.gov/

Organization of Women in International Trade
Website: www.owit.org

Small Business Administration's International Trade Loans
Website: www.sba.gov/services/financialassistance/sbaloantopics/
    specialpurposeloans/tradeloans/index.html

The Association of Women in International Trade
1707 L Street NW, Suite 570
Washington, DC 20036
Phone: 202-293-2948
Website: www.wiit.org

Legal Counsel

The Association of Black Women Attorneys
847A Second Avenue, Box 305
New York, NY 10017
Phone: 212-332-0748
Website: www.geocities.com/abwagroup

The National Conference of Black Lawyers
116 W. 111th Street
New York, NY 10027
Phone: 866-266-5091
Website: www.ncbl.org

Nolo's Lawyer Directory
Phone: 877-NOLO LAW
Website: www.lawyers.nolo.com

Life Matters/Personal Growth

Reposition Yourself: Living Life Without Limits by T. D. Jakes (2007)

Having What Matters: The Black Woman's Guide to Creating the Life You Really Want by Monique Greenwood (2001)

One Month to Live: Thirty Days to a No-Regrets Life by Kerry and Chris Shook (2008)

Iyanla Vanzant

Inner Visions Worldwide Network Inc and Bookstore

Phone: 310-419-8085

Website: www.innervisionsworldwide.com

In the Spirit: The Inspirational Writings of Susan L.taylor (2004)

Marketing

U.S. Patent and Trademark Office

Commissioner for Trademarks

PO Box 1451

Alexandria, VA 22313-1451

Website: www.uspto.gov

The Brand Called You: The Ultimate Personal Branding Handbook to Transform Anyone into an Indispensible Brand by Peter Montoya with Tim Vendehey (2005)

Black Speakers Online

Phone: 310-671-7136

Website: www.blackspeakers.net

Velvet Suite Marketing Group

Melissa D. Johnson, president

3340 Peachtree Road NE, Suite 1800

Atlanta, GA 30326

Phone: 404-806-8214

Website: www.velvetsuitemarketing.com

Frasernet.com (a global leadership network for black professionals)

George Fraser, CEO

SuccessGuide: The Networking Guide to Black Resources by George C. Fraser

Success Runs in Our Race: The Complete Guide to Networking in the Community by George C. Fraser (2004)

Small Business Branding

Website: www.smallbusinessbranding.com

Internet Marketing by Charles F. Hofacker (2000)

Guerrilla Marketing: Easy and Inexpensive Strategies for Making Big Profits from Your Small Business by Jay Conrad Levinson (2007)

Manufacturing

National Minority Supplier Development Council

1040 Avenue of the Americas, 2nd Floor

New York, NY 10018

Phone: 212-944-2430

Website: www.nmsdc.com

Personal Consulting Services

African American Therapists

Website: www.africanamericantherapists.com

Chicago's High Achievers (counseling services)

1330-B 127th Street

Calumet Park, IL 60827

Phone: 708-489-2265

Fax: 708-489-2176

E-mail: info@getting-better.net

Website: www.getting-better.net

Harriette Cole Productions (presentation training/image
    consulting)
10 W. 15th Street, Suite 526
New York, NY 10011
Phone: 212-645-3005
Fax: 212-206-3904
E-mail: contact@harriettecole.com
Website: www.harriettecole.com

Small Business Coaching
Small Business Camp
Phone: 914-633-0725
Website: www.90dayplan.com
KTD Coaching Services
Dr. Barbara Walton
Website: www.knowthedifference.com
International Coach Federation
Website: www.coachfederation.com
Quintessence Multimedia
A Strategic Communications Firm
67 Long Lane, Suite 130
Upper Darby, PA 19082
Phone: 610-532-0680
Fax: 610-532-0687
E-mail: info@quintessenceinc.com
Website: www.quintessenceinc.com
The Worldwide Association of Business Coaches
Website: www.wabccoaches.com

Tax Information

Internal Revenue Service

U.S. Department of the Treasury

Phone: 800-829-4933

Website: www.irs.gov

Trade Shows

www.TSNN.com (trade show event search tool)

Trade Show in a Day: Get It Done Right, Get It Done Fast! by Rhonda
    Abrams (2006)

How to Get the Most Out of Trade Shows by Steve Miller (2000)

CPSIA information can be obtained
at www.ICGtesting.com
Printed in the USA
LVHW111917161221
706400LV00012B/271